Signs, Wonders, and Worship
TOOLS OF THE END-TIME HARVEST

DAVID HARRIS

DESTINY IMAGE® PUBLISHERS, INC.

P.O. Box 310, Shippensburg, PA 17257-0310

"Speaking to the Purposes of God for this Generation and for the Generations to Come."

This book and all other Destiny Image, Revival Press, Mercy Place, Fresh Bread, Destiny Image Fiction, and Treasure House books are available at Christian bookstores and distributors worldwide.

For a U.S. bookstore nearest you, call 1-800-722-6774.
For more information on foreign distributors, call 717-532-3040.
Or reach us on the Internet: www.destinyimage.com.

ISBN 10: 0-7684-2505-0
ISBN 13: 978-0-7684-2505-5

Previously published by David C. Harris as ISBN 1-59872-235-2

For Worldwide Distribution, Printed in the U.S.A.

1 2 3 4 5 6 7 8 9 10 11 / 09 08 07

Dedication

This book is dedicated to the King of kings and the Lord of lords; to the Way (the gate), the Truth (the living Word personified), and the Life (abundant and everlasting)—Jesus Christ.

Acknowledgment

Many thanks to my niece, Amy Sadosky, without whom this book would have never been accomplished. Thank you, Amy, for your faithfulness, for being available at a moment's notice to work on this book with me. Your tireless dedication was priceless!

Big love,
Uncle David

Endorsements

This book is rife with the precious promise of the release of God's anointing on His Church. The prophetic dreams and visions that have been given to David and Judy Harris are powerful messages in themselves, but they also carry a weighty release of Divine purpose as they are drawn together in the message of this book. I know David and Judy. They are some of the most precious, real servants that I know. They constantly push through to the real and unreligious, and in so doing, they have garnered not only my affection, but also the affections of many who are tired of playing church games. More importantly, I believe that they have the affection and favor of God as they pursue the destiny of God for His people in New England and beyond.

Danny Steyne
Mountain of Worship
Columbia, South Carolina

On the landscape of history we see the shipwrecks of countless revivals and their associated religious dispensations. Occasionally, a light will shine in the darkness and an individual or ministry will escape the treacherous shores of tradition. David Harris is one of these individuals. He stands out like a lighthouse amidst a sea of repetitive verbiage and lifts up a clarion call of God's heart. David isn't just a "worshiper"; he knows *how* to worship. I pray that David's book, *Signs, Wonders, and Worship*, will take us into a revolutionary place of revival where the world will be changed because of it.

Chad Taylor
Author, *Why Revival Still Tarries*
www.consumingfire.com

This book not only speaks of the signs of the times, but is a trumpet proclaiming to the Bride—make your-self ready, prepare the way…

Brian Simmons

Many people have not had the privilege of hearing the revelations God has given to David; Contained herein, the articulation…

Wayne C. Anderson

Contents

Foreword

The Lord loves to share secrets with His friends. The deepest dreams of His heart are entrusted to the ones He loves the most. James 4:8 says, "Draw close to God and He will draw close to you…" (NLT). Those who diligently seek the Lord will find Him. God shares the secrets of His heart with those who are devoted to Him.

My friend David is a worshiper of God, a lover of the Most High. Every time I am in a service where he is leading worship, I can only imagine that the passion with which he sings comes from long, deep, and secluded times alone with God. David is my friend, but even more, he is a friend of God's. And like friends do, God has shared some of His secrets with David. The Lord gave David the revelation recorded in this book for a purpose. God has an agenda for every desire that He puts into our hearts. It is an assignment for us. The apostle Paul received revelation from God when he was taken to Heaven, and He waited fourteen years before he shared it with anyone else (2 Cor. 12:1-4), but some things are time-sensitive, and fresh manna for today. The message in this book is timely…it is beautiful. It is for the victorious Bride that the Lord is calling forth.

I know the ache that David carries to see the harvest come in, because it is in my heart also. God has placed common burdens in the hearts of many people throughout the Body at this time. There is a remnant praying to see the desires of God's heart manifested on the earth. Their prayers cry out to God to see all men come to know Jesus. Their shouts declare that this is the time for the Bride of Christ to be awakened to her destiny, to her full calling. There is a remnant ushering in the return of the King by proclaiming the gospel to every nation, tribe, and tongue. Men and women in our time are being raised up as eunuchs to prepare the Bride and to make her ready for her King. David is a part of that company, and this book comes from his heart to see these things come forth.

Ever since the Lord poured out his Spirit in the book of Acts, His Church has been growing and preparing for the Day of the Lord. The Lord promised in Joel 2:28-29, "Then after [I have poured out My rains again], I will pour out My Spirit upon all people. Your sons and daughters will prophesy. Your old men will dream dreams; your young men will see visions. In those days, I will pour out My Spirit even on servants, men and women alike" (NLT). This book not only speaks of the signs of the times, but it is also a trumpet proclaiming to the Bride, "Make yourself ready, prepare the way. You have a great task ahead. You have been called by God."

There is a day coming when every knee will bow and every tongue will confess. People near to you, who you never thought would call upon the name of Jesus, will shout it from the rooftops. Though in days past we have waited years, maybe even decades, to see visions fulfilled, today we live in a time of acceleration when the visions of God are being activated for immediate delivery. Get ready, God is pouring out His Spirit at high speeds. There is a harvest coming. It is coming through open vessels, open gates like David. It is making its way through men and women who are willing to be gates. Enter into this book, and dive into the revelation of *Signs, Wonders, and Worship.*

Brian Simmons
Senior Pastor
Gateway Christian Fellowship
West Haven, Connecticut

Preface

Before I begin the main message of this book, I would like to inform you of some assumptions and definitions that I use throughout the text. I hope this will assist your understanding as the Spirit guides you through this book.

First, in my discussion of the Tabernacle of David, I am not suggesting in any way that the restoration of the Tabernacle of David includes recreating the original music or format of King David's time. Our focus is to follow the Holy Spirit and to seek out the river of life in worship as we mingle with Heaven and converge with God's heart. We look for His River to flood the banks of our lives and cause a great gathering of worshipers to assemble:

> *I will surely assemble, O Jacob, all of thee; I will surely gather the remnant of Israel; I will put them together as the sheep of Bozrah, as the flock in the **midst of their fold**: they shall make great noise by reason of the multitude of men* (Micah 2:12).

These will gather with a great crescendo of power, drawing the lost into His salvation and the sick and maimed into His healing.

Second, throughout this book, I describe a spirit of religion whose function is to rob the Church of true worship. I have great disdain for anything that chokes out spiritual life. "Pure religion and undefiled before God and the Father is this, to visit the fatherless and widows in their affliction, and to keep himself unspotted from the world" (James 1:27 KJV). This is the only example of pure religion as defined from God's point of view in the entire Bible. All other forms of religion are a direct reflection of man's appetite for carnal reasoning. By definition, such reasoning creates a vacancy of genuine spiritual cognizance and revelation. God's word works for me. *Webster's* definition of *religious* is "being *bound* by vows of poverty."[1] God makes it very clear in His word that making a vow is evil. He says to let your yes be yes and your no be no; anything more than this is from the evil one, especially poverty (see James 5:12).

Third, I will refer to the end-times in this book in a way that will challenge traditional thought. Any time that I mention the *end-times* or the *last days* in relationship to the generation in which *we now live*, I am specifically referring to the fact that we have entered into the *times* when the *end* of natural history as we know it is at hand and when the return of our Lord is imminent. The *induction* of the millennial reign looms large. I have used the literal interpretation of Scripture to compile these teachings.

I hope that the revelation of true and spiritual worship and of God's absolute truth in Christ will be imparted to all who read this book. Let the reader find genuine relationship with the eternal lover of our souls, Jesus!

Introduction

We can belong to a "free" church, according to the standards we define as "free," and yet still exist in a variety of bondages. In fact, the standards that we use to define freedom become bondage, because standards cannot be lived up to. This is the very reason Jesus died. He satisfied the standard for us, because we could never do it on our own. It's all about the gospel of grace. Only God's word can define *freedom*, which is really found in the *grace* of God. If we are not inundated in the grace of God, we can find ourselves perplexed by a host of deceptions that are designed to keep us from experiencing the full gospel message of Christ. If salvation begins with believing His word, then why do we stray from His gospel of grace and fall into our own cookie cutter patterns of Church-ology?

The Lord has a plan to reform His Church and to restore the revelation of His gospel of grace to every believer. I am convinced that, as we move upon the face of an increasingly turbulent world, there will be an anointing to walk in faith like never before. Faith-fueled works, built upon a foundation of love, will change entire communities when the Body comes together *as one*.

The Church must come into a reformed and mature state in order to handle the battles ahead. I tell you that the day is coming, and is already here, when the denominations will be shaken, and from this shaking shall come the wheat, the true believers.

Jesus' prayer in John 17 will surely be answered. The diverse people of God have tried relentlessly for the last few decades to answer this prayer through ecumenical outreach and religious programs. It's as if the Church at large has manufactured an ecumenical reform pill in order to have everyone agree on the basic doctrines of salvation, believing that this alone is some semblance of unity. I tell you, until the whole Church is alive and empowered by the Holy Spirit, there will not be complete unity. Jesus Christ is not a doctrine; He is our living God! There is coming a day when the sword of the Lord will bring absolute distinction between the living Church and the dead wood. The wheat and the chaff will no longer exist together (see Matt. 3:12).

My friend and comrade in the ministry, Danny Steyne, delivered a prophetic word concerning these things. Part of what he said is this:

> In 1982, I had a dream about a giant that was asleep in a little white country church. The hand of the Lord came down and grabbed the shoulder of the giant and woke him up from his slumber. The giant stood up, and as he did, the building was shredded to bits. The Lord then spoke to me that there would be a day when the Church would stand, and there would be no structure; (neither religious, organizational, denominational, nor any other structure) that would be able to contain it. I believe we are witnessing the beginning of the disintegration of those structures. Millions have left the structures and are

unwilling to serve structures again…I believe these are the forerunners and in the coming days they will provide a multitude of prototype events intended on reflecting the glory of the Son.[2]

The only structure that will exist in the coming years will be according to Ephesians 2:19-22:

Now, therefore, you are no longer strangers and foreigners, but fellow citizens with the saints and members of the household of God, having been built on the foundation of the apostles and prophets, Jesus Christ Himself being the chief cornerstone, in whom the whole building, being fitted together, grows into a holy temple in the Lord, in whom you also are being built together for a dwelling place of God in the Spirit (NKJV).

Genuine reformation is upon the Church today, a reformation that is designed by the Lord according to the purposes of His heart from the very beginning. A Bride without spot or wrinkle is rising, a Bride with eyes as a dove, fixed upon the King of Kings (see Song of Sol. 1:15). The love of Christ is being shed abroad in our hearts, and no height nor depth, nor anything else in all of creation can separate us from the love of God which is in Christ Jesus our Lord (see Rom. 8:38-39). This love is the super glue that holds us together. This love is the very power that will bring the denominations crashing down and bring the true wheat together in harmony with the Lord and one another.

I tell you that an out-pouring of the Holy Spirit in these last days of natural history will release the love of Christ in unprecedented power, producing a unity that will bring the Bride of Christ back together again *as one*. The religious structures of old will be left for the antichrist spirit and will become like kindling. The enemy wants our religion, and he can have it and burn with it as well. As this all unfolds, the true Bride of Christ and the true worshipers of God will be empowered by the Holy Spirit in greater numbers to spread the manifest love of Christ. Truly, they will know that we are Christians by our love (see John 13:34). After many years, the reformed and unified body of Christ will arise and shine like a diamond upon the backdrop of a dark and dying world, and the testimony of this unity will be our diadem.

Contained within this book are teachings concerning the continuing reformation of the Church, the restoration of the Tabernacle of David, a brief history of the Church since renewal broke out in January of 1994, explanations of God's sifting process in choosing His victorious remnant of last days worship warriors (army of Gideon), explanations of the numbers *seven* and *three* and their significance in biblical prophecy of the Day of the Lord, an overview of the Day of the Lord, and a revelatory scenario of how the Lord Himself views the glory of His Great Day just prior to His return, as it was revealed in a dream and confirmed in the Scriptures.

So strap in! This easy-to-read book is packed with vital information. It's my prayer that those who read this book will be further equipped with faith to persevere in what *God* is doing, and with holy patience to wait on God like the living creatures in Ezekiel chapter 1, who moved only with the Spirit and kept the burning fire of their holy torches glowing. I also pray for those who don't know the Lord and read this book, hoping that the unusual nature of these writings will be unlike anything they have ever heard and will usher them into a deep heart conviction for Christ. Lord, may this book be a doorkeeper, ushering *all* into a new life and freedom in You.

Chapter 1

Harvest at Gate Beautiful

A mighty harvest is waiting at the gate, and the Lord is especially passionate for this one, just as He longed to share Passover with His disciples before He was crucified. The very *fullness* of time is upon us, and Heaven's reaping angels are ready and eager to release power and gather the harvest from the four corners of the earth. Worship will soon find its way out into the streets, and the public courtyards will become the place for the Lord to manifest His presence over us. You might wonder why this hasn't already happened. For instance, why didn't The Call wind up manifesting a full blown revival? The answer is that God has a perfect and absolute time to release it. Until then, we need to be obedient and continue in the Lord with anointed movements like The Call.[1]

This chapter will reveal the reality of the perfect timing of God. We do not know the hour of this great revival, but we know that it is very close at hand. We must be continuously ready for it. We must keep our lamps trimmed (see Matt. 25:1-13). There is no time like the present to worship the Lord in spirit and in truth (see John 4:23).

The Dream

The Lord speaks to us in very absolute ways. For me, He usually tells me something I don't know anything about, and then He tells me to look it up, and when I do, a world of revelation flows over me like a flood. It's wonderful to have a God that wants us to be aware of Him and alert to His perfect will. One time, the Lord told my wife Judith in a dream that He was waiting for her at Gate Beautiful. Because of the unusual nature of this message, it was necessary to do some research. In so doing, I discovered the following information. The Gate Beautiful was the entrance to the public courtyard of the temple. The lame beggar that Jesus healed through Peter entered the Beautiful Gate with thanksgiving and entered the courtyard with praise (see Acts 3:1-10). This beggar is a sign of when the multitudes will "enter into His gates with thanksgiving...and into His courts with praise..." (Ps. 100:4).

So why do you suppose the Lord said, "I'm waiting for you at Gate *Beautiful?*" First of all, we are now the gates. Psalm 87:2 says, "The Lord loves the gates of Zion [through which the crowds of pilgrims enter from all nations] more than all the dwellings of Jacob (Israel)." Several verses later, it says:

> *Yes, of Zion it shall be said, this man and that man were born in her, for the Most High Himself will establish her. The Lord shall count, when He registers the peoples, that this man was born there. Selah* [pause and calmly think of that]*! The singers as well as the players on instruments shall say, all my springs (my sources of life and joy) are in you [city of our God]* (Psalm 87:5-7).

Similarly, Psalm 24:7 says, "Lift up your *heads*, O you gates; and be lifted up, you age-abiding doors, that the King of glory may come in." As these verses demonstrate, we are the gates.

The key of David (spiritual worship) is what opens these human gates. Shouting doctrine from the roof tops is no longer effective. The soil of the human heart will be cultivated by the Holy Spirit through the anointing of prophetic worship. The temple was a place of worship, but we are now the worshiping temple, and the Lord Jesus dwells within. The gate was a place of entrance to the temple court, and we are now the gates through whom the pilgrims enter into God's presence. The courtyard was the public meeting place of the temple, and the public arena is where we will go with the praises of the Lord.

So, for the Lord to say that He awaits us at Gate Beautiful implies that we will be going to the public courtyards as a temple of worshiping gates that are wide open for the Lord. As He comes, the lost will enter through these gates and encounter Jesus. What an awesome privilege it will be to usher in the great harvest through the intimate wedlock of intercession and worship. Jesus Himself will be the great evangelist. Miracles, signs, and wonders will follow in the wake of this anointed worship, and multitudes of spiritual orphans will receive salvation.

But why was the gate called *beautiful*? It wasn't called beautiful because it was arrayed with gold and fine craftsmanship. The word *beautiful* in Acts 3:2 was translated from the Greek word *horaios* and means "belonging to the right hour or season (timely); a *day* or hour, high time."[2] This season of the Lord's power will be like a freeze-frame of timely glory. God will move by His Spirit more powerfully than ever before in these final days of human history. In His own *beautiful* time, He will move through the gates of Zion in order to possess the remnant of Edom and all of the nations that are called by His name. Our holy quarterback (Jesus) will throw the ball to His wide receivers (the Gates of Zion) at the exact nanosecond when the enemy is caught off guard, resulting in the most graceful Lynn Swann, one-handed, fingertip touchdown reception of all time: a thing of beauty![3] The glory of God will touch down; yes, the knowledge of the glory of the Lord will fill the earth as the waters cover the sea (see Hab. 2:14).

In the chapters to come we will discover the awesome timing of the Lord, His perfect and beautiful timing for the grand finale of this present age. From the time that the Lord said, "Let there be light," till this very moment, a masterfully designed plan for redemption and matrimony has unfolded. The fullness of time has arrived, and we have entered into the "*Day* of the Lord." Let your God-given imagination take you into a fantastic realm of expectation as you turn these pages. Discover who you are in Christ and who Christ is in you. Find out why you are restless and hungry for more and more of Him, and why nothing but Him will ever satisfy you. The Lord is wooing His Bride out of the wilderness; and here she comes, out of that wilderness, leaning on her Beloved (see Song of Sol. 8:3).

CHAPTER 2

The Restoration of the Tabernacle of David

Remarkable parallels exist between the Tabernacle of David, as described in the Scriptures, and the prophetic promise of the Lord to reap the last great harvest in the days that lie just ahead. The hearts of the modern-day Levites are thrilled at the prospect of ushering in the presence of the Lord in the public places of their cities.

There are prophetic and apostolic round tables that meet regularly to discuss and pray about the intentions of the Lord for revival, but one very crucial element is missing from these discussions: the Levites. Worship will be our biggest weapon in the battle, but currently the worshipers are stuck in a holding pattern. The key of David (spiritual worship) must be loosed from its bonds and allowed to open the holy gates of Heaven in the earth. The apostolic government of God must begin to include the apostolic worship leaders and prophetic lightning rods of the Lord. There must be a marriage between the preaching ministries and the worship ministries.

In this chapter, we will take a look at types and shadows found within the ministry of David. The Lord prophesied about the Church of this day through David, calling us all into a prophetic, royal priesthood. All of His children are called as prophets, priests, and kings. No wonder worship comes under the most vicious attacks from the enemy. When the Church releases the revelation of Christ through worship, there will be nothing holding back power for the harvest. Perpetual prophetic and regal priestly ministry unto the Lord must become a mandate for the Church in this hour.

Let's look at the Scriptures that form the foundation of the Tabernacle of David. Acts 15:13-18 says:

When they had finished talking, James replied, "Brethren, listen to me. Simeon [Peter] has rehearsed how God first visited the Gentiles, to take out of them a people [to bear and honor] His name. And with this the predictions of the prophets agree, as it is written, 'After this I will come back, and will rebuild the house of David, which has fallen; I will rebuild its [very] ruins, and I will set it up again, So that the rest of men may seek the Lord, and all the Gentiles upon whom My name has been invoked,' says the Lord, who has been making these things known from the beginning of the world."

Here we see that James is prophesying about the Gentiles. He speaks as if the Tabernacle of David is about to be restored in the immediate future. This is the nature of prophesy; he sees the end result and declares it as if it were ready to manifest. He said, "After this…." After what? After the Lord *first* visits the Gentiles, then He would come and rebuild the Tabernacle of David. In Acts, the Lord had just begun to move upon the Gentiles and would continue to do so for the next 2,000 plus years.

Also in Amos 9:11-12 it says:

The Restoration of the Tabernacle of David

"In that day will I raise up the tabernacle of David, the fallen hut or booth, and close up its breaches; and I will raise up its ruins, and I will build it as in the days of old, that they may possess the remnant of Edom and of all the nations that are called by My name," says the Lord who does this.

Verse 14 of the same passage goes on to say, "And I will bring back the exiles of My people Israel..." and verse 15 says, "And I will plant them upon their land...." Here in Amos, God declares, "In that day...." In what day? The day when He brings back the exiles of His people Israel and plants them upon their land; this is the day that He will raise up the Tabernacle of David. My friends, we are *in that day*—a day which is fast approaching, which is the fullness of time. It is the Day of the Lord! Both of these Scriptures are being fulfilled. The global Church is largely a Gentile Church, and the Jews are poised to reclaim their home-land Israel. Although they already inhabit a portion of the prom-ise, even now, a massive threat to declare war against them is imminent. However, God has a plan for the Jews to come into their full inheritance, and as this is realized, the Tabernacle of David will be restored, and the remnant of Jews and Gentiles will be called into the Kingdom.

In these days, we look for the fulfillment of Ezekiel 37:19, which says,

Behold, I will take the stick of Joseph—which is in the hand of **Ephraim**—*and the tribes of Israel his associates, and will join with it the stick of Judah and make them one stick, and they shall be* **one** *in My hand.*

Jew and Gentile shall be made one and become a united nation (Holy Israel). Jacob (Israel) demonstrates this in Genesis when he claims Ephraim and Manasseh (who were half-Gentile and half-Jew) as his *adopted* sons. And He states that all who are born after them shall bear their name when they come into their inheritance.

> *And now your two sons, [Ephraim and Manasseh], who were born to you in the land of Egypt before I came to you in Egypt, are mine. [I am adopting them, and now] as Reuben and Simeon, [they] shall be mine. But other sons who may be born after them shall be your own; and they shall be called after the names of these [two] brothers and reckoned as belonging to them [when they come] into their inheritance* (Genesis 48:5-6).

Later, Jacob (Israel) says that Ephraim's off-spring shall become a multitude of nations. Speaking of Manasseh, he says, "…His younger brother [Ephraim] shall be greater than he, and his offspring shall become a multitude of nations (Gen. 48:19). Here the Gentiles are claimed as God's inheritance through Israel's act of adopting them as sons. They enter spiritual adoption through Israel the man and Israel the nation. This is what God prophesied through Ezekiel—Ephraim holds the stick of Joseph and joins that stick with the stick of Judah, making them one in the hand of the Lord. We are closing in on the days of this prophesy, when Jew and Gentile will become one new man.

Thy Kingdom Come

Consider the Lord's Prayer. Jesus didn't give us this prayer as a nice little bedtime story for our children. He said that we should pray, "Thy kingdom come…" (Matt. 6:10 KJV). God's Kingdom is His authority to rule and reign. When we worship in spirit and in truth (see John 4:23), we establish the rule and reign of the Lord in the earth. We become empowered by the Holy Spirit to take the land, the harvest fields. The soil is prepared. The furrows are dug, and the seed of His word of truth is deposited into the fertile soil of the human heart. This brings us to the next line of the prayer Jesus taught us: "thy will be done." When we enter into agreement with God in this type of intimate and prophetic worship, we literally become pregnant in our spiritual womb as His Bride in the earth. In this place, we enter travailing labor until His desires come to pass.

Finally the punch line of the Lord's Prayer: "in earth as it is in heaven." Birthing spiritual life in the earth is one specific purpose of intimacy with God through worship. When a man and woman lay together in marriage, they produce children. However, this is not the only reason they lay together. They desire one another. They literally become one in their union. God has an insatiable desire for us, just as we do for Him. This is not gross sexual imagery. Rather, God uses this imagery in Scripture, saying that the marriage bed is a mystery concerning Christ and the Church (see Eph. 5:31-32). It is also a pale version of the kind of spiritual intimacy that we can *already* have with Him now, if we want it.

In these last days, The Lord will introduce into the earth the realities of Heaven through love-sick prophetic worship, and all the earth will be filled with the knowledge of the glory of the Lord. "Thy kingdom come, Thy will be done in earth, as it is in Heaven." This is the nature of David's Tabernacle. It provided a type and a shadow of Heaven's worship in the earth, and it provided a habitation of the Lord, where all could come into His presence. What a perfect prayer for the Lord to give us. God will create, through *worship*, a public mercy seat, His holy habitation. There is a season which is fast approaching when God will anoint worship to usher in waves of His power to flood the cities with His glory.

Shadows of the Fathers

The ark of the Lord landed at Abinadab's house after its exodus through the enemy's camp:

> *Again David gathered together all the chosen men of Israel, 30,000. And [he] arose and went with all the people who were with him to Baale-judah [Kiriath-jearim] to bring up from there the ark of God, which is called by the name of the Lord of hosts, Who sits enthroned above the cherubim. And they set the ark of God upon a new cart and brought it out of the house of Abinadab, which was on the hill; and Uzzah and Ahio, sons of Abinadab, drove the new cart* (2 Samuel 6:1-3).

David retrieved the ark of the Lord from Abinadab with the intention of bringing it home. *Abinadab* means "to offer freely and to volunteer willingly."[1] Abinadab held onto the ark, but when it was time, he willingly released it, charging his two sons to go with David and drive the new cart. Abinadab was from Baale of Judah, which means "to lord over and to be master of [Judah]."[2] The Church of today has held Judah (praise) in bonds and has lorded over it, but the true fathers of the Church will willingly release it go with the David's of this era. The job of the true fathers has been to equip and release the sons of David in this generation. Malachi prophesied, "And he [the spirit of Elijah] will turn the hearts of the fathers to the children, and the hearts of the children to their fathers, lest I come and strike the earth with a curse" (Mal. 4:6 NKJV).

Like Abinadab, the fathers have guarded and nurtured the ark of the Lord for a season. But now they are sending the David's of this generation to take the worship outside of the four walls. When David came with his troops, they took the ark from

Abinadab's house and hit the streets with it, but something happened along the way:

> And when they came to Nacon's threshing floor, Uzzah put
> out his hand to the ark of God and took hold of it, for the oxen
> stumbled and shook it. And the anger of the Lord was kindled
> against Uzzah; and God smote him there for touching the ark,
> and he died there by the ark of God (2 Samuel 6:6-7).

We all know the story of Uzzah, who tried to steady the ark as the oxen stumbled across the threshing floor. We are going to stumble a bit sometimes when we are carrying the glory to the heartlands. However, when we come to the threshing floors of our cities, we are not to get in the way and try to bring fleshly order to the worship of the Lord. God will not have any more of that, to be sure. Uzzah's attempt to steady the ark of the Lord is a picture of man trying to steer and direct God's glory. Believe me, God's glory will take care of itself.

After Uzzah was struck down by the Lord, David sent the ark to Obed-Edom's house. After David received word that Obed-Edom was being mightily blessed, he went back to claim it again. David retrieved the ark of the Lord and brought it into Jerusalem, dancing through the streets as they went and slaughtering an ox and a fatling every six paces. Can you imagine the cost of such offerings? I haven't done the math, but you can be sure that an unimaginable number of oxen and fatlings were sacrificed. This kind of an offering was nothing compared to the awesome perpetual presence of the Lord that inhabited the city of David. There was no veil in David's Tabernacle, which allowed *all* people to come into the presence of God's glory. Tell me, how much is that worth? Don't even dare put a number on it! This is what we shall enjoy once again at the Beautiful Gate (the perfect timing of

God), when He will pour out an unprecedented wave of His power.

To see a sustained habitation of the Lord in our cities is a task that demands serious corporate commitment. It demands unity of mind, heart, and purpose with God and one another; it also demands a wave of selfless, sacrificial giving. I will say that again: a corporate and regional habitation of God's Spirit demands unity of mind, heart, and purpose with *selfless*, sacrificial giving! When the Lord begins to move in power, it will be *our* turn to respond to Him. Thankfully, there *will* come a time when His people will give of themselves *willingly* in the day of His power. As Psalm 110:3 says, "Your people will offer themselves willingly in the day of Your power, in the beauty of holiness and in holy array out of the womb of the morning; to You [will spring forth] Your young men, who are as the dew."

The Levites (worship leaders) *must* be called back from the fields (the secular workplace) into full-time holy service, ministering to the Lord. When the Lord blows the trumpets of revival, the Body of Christ will need to respond if they expect God to sustain a habitation of His presence. This kind of permanent revival, which brings a marked change in the entire community, must be fueled by a radical and permanent wave of sacrificial giving that will sustain the needs of the Levites, who are to be exclusively separated unto the Lord. As true spiritual and prophetic worship is rebuilt world-wide, the Church, endowed with power, will arise as prophesied. Miracles, signs, and wonders will follow in the wake of her love-sick spiritual worship. The golden bowls will become full (see Rev. 5:8), and judgment mingled with grace shall break out. The Lord will judge sickness and disease, and the grace for healing will be the result. The Lord will judge sin (not sinners), and the grace for salvation will be the result. The Lord will judge religion, and the grace for an outpouring of His Spirit and the habitation of the Lord in our cities will be the result.

This activity will include worshipers and intercessors from every denomination and from every *previous* walk of faith. I use the term *previous* because the Lord is going to shake His Church. The molds of religion shall be broken, releasing forerunners from every denomination for this work. You see, this is a *Body-wide* pruning which will result in true oneness. Very soon we will *all* be of one mind and purpose. We will have one function (the Great Commission), and one first love (the Lord). When all is said and done, we will be *One United Church!* We are *all* called to be a prophetic, royal priesthood. This unified, global Church of worship and prayer will have an anointing to reveal the salvation of Christ and to display an intimate spiritual love affair between God and His people. In these times, look for the glory cloud to manifest. Look for signs and wonders that will frustrate the enemy and spark delight in the hearts of new believers everywhere!

A House of Living Stones

God commanded David, through Gad the seer, to set up an altar to the Lord on the threshing floor of Ornan the Jebusite. "Then the angel of the Lord commanded Gad to say to David that David should go up and set up an altar to the Lord in the threshing floor of Ornan the Jebusite. So David went up at Gad's word, which he spoke in the name of the Lord" (1 Chron. 21:18-19). Because David was of the tribe of Judah, not Levi, he was technically disqualified from offering sacrifices, according to the law at that time; yet God commanded the sacrifice on Mount Moriah and consumed it with fire. By allowing David to sacrifice, though he was not technically of the priestly tribe, God gave a sign of the time to come when all of His Bride would be priests unto Him.

Also, by allowing David to build an altar outside of the traditional place of sacrifice (the tabernacle of Moses), God gave a sign of the time to come when worship would take on a new form and expression that would not be limited by a religious format. These events prophesied the Church's release from the law and entrance into grace.

While the Lord prophetically made these end-times declarations through David, He also gave David the revelation to build the temple on the threshing floor of Ornan the Jebusite on Mount Moriah (which is where Abraham brought Isaac as a sacrifice to the Lord). "Then David said, 'Here shall be the house of the Lord God, and here the altar of the burnt offering for Israel.' David commanded to gather together the strangers who were in the land of Israel, and he set stone cutters to hew out stones to build the house of God" (1 Chron. 22:1-2). Later we read about Solomon's fulfillment of David's vision for the temple. "Then Solomon began to build the house of the Lord at Jerusalem on Mount Moriah, where the Lord appeared to David his father, in the place that David had appointed, on the threshing floor of Ornan the Jebusite" (2 Chron. 3:1).

This temple represented the city of God, the New Jerusalem (see Rev. 21:2-3), and mirrored as well, the completed Bride of Christ, who in these latter days of natural history, will gather together the great harvest in freedom and liberty from religion. The word *Jebusite* means "an inhabitant of Jebus," which means "threshing place." The threshing floor is a place of repentance as well as a place of sifting. It symbolically represents a place where the harvest will come to the salvation of the Lord. Jebus is also the aboriginal name of Jerusalem.[3] This is a very fitting place for a temple representing the *New* Jerusalem to be built. Further, I believe that this temple of worship, which was built on the threshing floor of Ornan the Jebusite, is a prophetic statement of the Lord. He declared that His habitation, or permanent dwelling, would be with men, which is a house of *living stones* (see 1 Pet. 2:5). As a temple of worship in the Day of the Lord, we will create a threshing floor where the lost will come in and be swept away in the worship of the Lord.

The day-and-night watch prescribed by the Lord in Scripture will again bring forth a type of throne room worship on the earth. The devil accuses us day and night, so we must also worship day and night:

> *I have set watchmen upon your walls, O Jerusalem, who will never hold their peace day or night; you who [are His servants and by your prayers] put the Lord in remembrance [of His promises], keep not silence, And give Him no rest until He establishes Jerusalem and makes her a praise in the earth* (Isaiah 62:6-7).

As Jesus said in Luke 18:7, "And will not [our just] God defend and protect and avenge His elect (His chosen ones), who cry to Him day and night? Will He defer them and delay help on their behalf?"

The veils of religion that we have all created must be removed. David's Tabernacle had no veil. He set up shop on the town green, and all could come before the glory of the Lord. Spiritual worship is an unhindered heart-to-heart communion between God and His people. It is an interaction of wedlock between the Divine Creator and His creation. Worship is more than a musical expression of affection for the Lord. Worship is a mutual interaction between His heart and ours. We beat in unity with the divine purposes of King Jesus. It is a lifestyle of being one with the Lord. We will see a corporate release of glory as we engage the wine press of Spirit-led worship in *unity*, releasing His heart over the nations. Let the roar of the Lord be heard from Zion! God loves the gates of Zion. He will count, when He registers the peoples, all those who were born there (see Psalm 87).

Also in First Chronicles 17:10b-12, the Lord spoke to David through the prophet Nathan:

> *I foretell to you that the Lord will build you a house (a blessed posterity). And it shall come to pass that when your days are fulfilled to go to be with your fathers, I will raise up your offspring after you, one of your own sons, and I will establish His kingdom. He shall build Me a house, and I will establish His throne forever.*

Then, in verse 14, He goes on to say, "But I will settle him (Him) in My house and in My kingdom forever, and (His) throne shall be established forevermore" (1 Chron. 17:14). Notice the capitalized parenthetical reference to "Him" in this verse. This shows that Jesus is the subject of this Scripture. The word *posterity* here means a few different things. It means the "last or end, the future, end time, remnant, and reward,"[4] it speaks of being a "dwelling and an evermore generation,"[5] and it also means "the offspring of one progenitor to the furthest generation and all future generations."[6] Thus, *posterity* speaks of our fixed heavenly dwelling and inheritance. The evermore generation is the mature Bride of Christ that will live out all of eternity with the Lord. Verse 12 says, *"He shall build Me a house…."* Solomon built the house in the natural, foreshadowing the perfected Bride of Christ and the New Jerusalem.

This temple prophetically mirrors the true and spiritual house of the Lord that Jesus is building. This house is built not by human hands but by Jesus Himself, because Jesus is the offspring of the one progenitor (King David) to the furthest generation and *all* future generations. Solomon built the house in the natural, but Jesus builds the house by His Spirit. The house is His Church, a house of living stones. Publicly demonstrated, fiery worship accompanied by miracles, signs, and wonders manifested in this house in these last days will bring in the lost from the four winds of the earth. In the midst of this, the Lord will knit unity into the fabric of His people. There will eventually be no more denominations, but only one unified Church. There will be a victorious "one new man" Church shortly before the return of Jesus, and there will be a very clear distinction between the Lord's camp and the enemy's camp. The enemy has it in mind to create a system revolving around *one world religion* that will be in direct defiance of the true Church of Christ. The living Church wants to throw off the shackles of religion altogether, and the enemy wants to snatch it up and use it for his purposes. Therefore, let him have it and let him burn with it!

The Scripture in Acts 15, which we discussed earlier, tells us very clearly that the restoration of the Tabernacle of David will come to pass so that the rest of men may seek the Lord. However, before the Lord could move on His people to initiate this work, He had to do a great deal of renovation. Indeed, He's been very busy gutting the house and starting from scratch. Only God can put asunder what God has joined. Only God has the wisdom to divide the many camps to multiply the *one true camp*. Construction is underway, and the closing date is on schedule!

CHAPTER 3

Divide the House To Multiply the House

Much has been said these days about the sudden nomadic movement among the Body of Christ. Pastors are getting uneasy and feeling a change in the spiritual climate. The flocks are uneasy in their pews, and everyone seems to be searching for the answer to this seemingly sudden dissatisfaction with church the way it has been. Are people in rebellion? Have they lost their sense of family? Do pastors even have the same authority that they used to have? Why have the sheep scattered? There are so many questions. Though there are many stable and flourishing congregations, there are as many that have tasted these bitter waters.

The Lord Himself has caused a great stirring among His worshipers. They must have more. Church politics can be an irritation and hinder worship, unless of course it is the church policy to encourage life and vitality in the worship. Those who have tasted *God-inhabited* worship need to express their love according to the movement of the Spirit, and they feel shut-down by calculated church programs. Why? Once you have tasted the waters of spiritual worship, and once you have delved into that well of freedom, it is impossible to be satisfied with anything that falls short of that. Show a child a play ground, and the play pen will become a prison. This is why many "play pen" churches are experiencing a shifting.

Church as we know it is being radically altered by the Spirit of the Lord. Judith and I have created a safe place for the regional nomads of the Church in New England, in response to the Lord. There must be a way for the faithful to gather. If they don't gather, then the faithful gathering will be forsaken. What *is* a safe environment for the freedom seekers? Well, *freedom*, of course, is the answer. The one who the Son sets free is free indeed (see John 8:36). If He has led captivity captive (see Eph. 4:8), then invite *Him* into your gatherings and you will have liberty. Truly, where the Spirit of the Lord is, there is genuine liberty (see 2 Cor. 3:17). We must learn to let the Holy Spirit determine the direction of our gatherings. Our meetings are not about worshiping the idea of the Lord. They are not for the purpose of talking about the Lord. They are all about encountering the living Lord in our midst and having *communion* with Him.

This chapter describes some of the work that the Lord has performed in order to bring His Bride into position to receive Him. What He really did was show up and interrupt our organized meetings. After that, many would settle for nothing less. The house of David is being restored, but like any old house in the natural, some demolition and renovations have to take place before the house can be restored to its original splendor. The Church, under the influence of the religious spirit, is like an old house, left unattended and allowed to deteriorate. When the carpenter Jesus shows up to rebuild the house, certain timbers of the house are dismantled and set aside because their structural integrity has severely diminished. Meanwhile, other timbers are restored, in order to be used strategically to re-establish the original design. The dismantled timbers are replaced with new ones that are fashioned according to the Lord's purposes, in order to fulfill His will.

The fresh anointing on worship (which was birthed in the 1994 renewal), has been continually redefining itself, going deeper and higher. This anointing has actually been used as a wrecking ball, through which the mold *breakers* frustrated the mold *makers*. When I say mold breakers, I'm referring to those worshiping "charismaniacs" who will settle for absolutely nothing less than the manifest presence of the Holy Spirit. In their zeal, these people have stepped all over the church program. And I believe that God *ordained* and anointed these people to step all over the church program.

But the mold *makers* (those who established the various diehard political agendas designed to cater to the flesh and keep God in a box) have brought out their heavy artillery in a *futile* attempt to shut down the movement of the Holy Spirit. The religious spirit and those who serve it *religiously* are a different cut of cloth from those who are simply duped by it. Those who are in consort with it are like dark clouds without water whose sole function is to block out the light of God's glory. They are like the men described in Jude:

> *For certain men have crept in stealthily [gaining entrance secretly by a side door]. Their doom was predicted long ago, ungodly (impious, profane) persons who pervert the grace (the spiritual blessing and favor) of our God into lawlessness and wantonness and immorality, and disown and deny our sole Master and Lord, Jesus Christ (the Messiah, the Anointed One)....These are hidden reefs (elements of danger) in your*

love feasts, where they boldly feast sumptuously [carousing together in your midst], without scruples providing for themselves [alone]. They are clouds without water, swept along by the winds; trees, without fruit at the late autumn gathering time—twice (doubly) dead, [lifeless and] plucked up by the roots (Jude 4,12).

These renegades of religiosity have built roofs upon their houses and installed facades designed to cover up the sin of their idolatry and self-made religious kingdoms. Roofs such as these cannot be easily removed, but they *must* be removed, and the Lord *is* removing them. Metaphorically speaking, God is removing the Pharaohs and those born of their religious kingdoms. The true worshipers of God will be released from the bondage of Egypt and spread out to worship the Lord as He fully intends and desires.

Every tribe, tongue, and nation will gather together in unity. True worshipers from every denomination will come together as one Bride to praise and worship in the power of the Holy Spirit and to "drink of victory, and to be noisy and turbulent" (Zech. 9:15). We shall usher in the commanded blessing over massive geographical regions, literally flooding the earth with the knowledge of the glory of the Lord as we worship Him in spirit and in truth. This is the very ministry that the religious spirit has been combating. It has actually been a war, and there have been casualties of this war, as evidenced by all the Church splits throughout the world. But I believe that, in the midst of all these splits, the Lord's plan is to *divide the many camps in order to multiply the one true camp.*

While the Lord has been manifesting many prophetic expressions of the Holy Spirit through His Body over the last thirteen years, He has also been using His Spirit of liberty in worship to divide His house. Only God can contrive such an idea, using the Spirit of freedom as a tool to divide. The Church in these days is definitely in the hands of the divine Potter. The Lord does not divide to tear asunder, like the enemy. When God divides, He does it so that those divided will spread abroad and multiply His truth. Through a corporate pruning, He brings more life. The Lord is exercising wisdom in a way that the carnal mind cannot justify. He's very busy frustrating the natural intellect of men. He loves to embarrass the proud and to exalt the humble. It is very evident that the *humble* will be used of God to *exalt Him* in the public arena. One who is humble receives from others with grace and gratitude, without making excuses for his gifting. Let those who are prepared to receive all that the Lord is ready to pour out, be set apart as gates for the glory of the Lord to shine through.

There is going to be a fresh and powerful outpouring of the Spirit, and a fresh host of manifestations will accompany it. Many physically unnatural events will occur. In the days to come, there will be crowds of worshipers so intensely intoxicated on His love and His electric presence that they will appear to be feigning mad. One of the seventeen different Hebrew words for "praise" is *halal*, which means "to rage and to feign mad."[1] When you or I find ourselves in the real presence of an electric, loving God, who is powerful enough to contain the entire universe, we might perhaps be so overcome by His joy that we seem to be feigning mad. Was the Lord prophesying of the time when His Church would enter into this kind of praise, or is the Hebrew language just that colorful? The psalmist describes dancers spinning violently like a top (see Ps. 9:14b). (This scripture and others will be dissected in the original language in chapter 6.) Could it be, that worshipers may find themselves dancing so violently, while weaving in and out of a crowd, that they seem to be completely out of control, yet they don't even intrude upon anyone else's space? One might look upon this as someone feigning mad. Sound far-fetched? This very dance manifestation has happened to my wife, Judith. We can learn a little something from our pets perhaps. Even my puppy feigns mad! When my puppy, Cody, sees me coming, he begins to leap and twirl violently, making yippy sounds of joy! My cat, Baboo, sees this and scowls at him like David's wife Michal (see 1 Chron. 15:29).

I believe that God will release these kinds of signs and wonders corporately in the days to come. Zechariah 9:13 says, "For I have bent Judah [praise and worship] for Myself as My bow [weapon], filled the bow with Ephraim [the nations] as My arrow...." (I have inserted the words in brackets to describe my interpretation of what this Scripture is saying.) This indicates that the Lord will use worship as His weapon against darkness, in order to win the nations. In the wedlock of worshiping our King, nothing can stand in the way of the spiritual reproduction of Heaven in the earth. Verse 14 goes on to say, "And the Lord shall be *seen* over them and His arrow shall go forth as the lightning..." (Zech. 9:14). The Lord will manifest Himself over us in these times, anointing our worship to bring in the last days harvest. He shall emerge through corporate prophetic worship: "...and they shall drink [of victory] and be noisy and turbulent as from wine and become full like bowls [used to catch the sacrificial blood], like the corners of the [sacrificial] altar" (Zech. 9:15).

He will pour out more and more of the wine of His presence as these Gate Beautiful revivals are released, and we shall drink of victory like never before. One cannot remain calm and appealingly appropriate to the carnal man when confronted by the living God. In these times ahead, we will fill the golden bowls with worship and intercession (see Rev. 5:8). All men will be drawn to the Lord because we will be proclaiming *His* sacrificial blood with an anointing unlike anything we have ever experienced before. You can expect this to be a noisy and turbulent scene of worship (see Zech. 9:15).

When the anointing of the Lord fell upon the Toronto Blessing conferences, which broke out in January of 1994, the movement was heavily persecuted. Granted, there were a lot of strange manifestations that were hard to explain, but they weren't impossible to explain since many of them are found in the Word of God, as we will continue to discover throughout this book. Furthermore, the fruit of the Holy Spirit is evident in the salvations and healings that frequently happened. Church leaders from all over the world attended those meetings, received impartation, and returned home to transfer this anointing throughout the earth and shake up the Church in the process. When the true power of God falls upon us and we yield to His presence and to the movement of the Holy Spirit, our human flesh manifests in many different ways. This has a two-fold effect. It frustrates the intellectual, Bible-thumping fundamentalist, and it mightily blesses the one who has been praying hard for a touch from Almighty God.

My friend and father in the faith, Wayne Anderson, was speaking to the Lord concerning some of the manifestations that were happening in the renewal, and he said, "Lord, You sure do some strange things to Your people." The Lord answered him and said, "No Wayne, My people sure do some strange things when I touch them." We can gather from this that not everything that happens in the wacky world of manifestations is a prophetic symbol from the Lord. Many of the manifestations are prophetic, but sometimes people are just responding as anyone would after putting their finger into a 220-volt electric socket. Signs and wonders (manifestations) follow those who are operating in the anointing of the Holy Spirit (see 2 Cor. 12:12). We don't idolize the gifts; we worship the gift-giver. These manifestations point to the work of the Holy Spirit among believers and are like a distinguishing mark.

It's no mistake that the anointing of the Holy Spirit, which has been producing *surface* manifestations of the power of God touching His people, would stir up such contention in the worldwide Church. There is a divine order to this. By instituting this freedom and bold expressiveness in worship, the Lord has been discerning who will follow the glory cloud and who will persecute the move of God. It's interesting that the Lord would use the freedom that He released in worship during the renewal as a wrecking ball in His own house. The spirit of religion was aroused, raising its ugly head in control, rebellion, and unbelief, for the first time in a long time. Meanwhile, worship took on new strength in the name of freedom, submission, and pure belief. With a fresh wave of intimacy in worship, He interrupted the programs of dead works and self-righteousness to frustrate the religious spirit with the revelation of grace. It is the kindness of God that draws us to repentance (see Rom. 2:4). In these times, the Lord will woo His Bride out of the wilderness of religion and into a saucy lover's relationship that has scarcely been realized in the Church. Mysteries of God that have long been hidden will be revealed and the Bride of Christ will arise and shine!

CHAPTER 4

The Army of Gideon

From the ranks of reformation rises a new breed of worshipers. The reformation of the Church has only just begun, but charging from the gate is a small army of radical forerunners that I like to call Gideon's army—a focused regiment of unsettled nomads. These so-called rebels are hunting for that anointed place where they can drive their stake into the land and claim it for the glory of the Lord. Nothing short of a habitation of the Lord will satisfy them. The renewal produced fruit in many ways, especially in the battlefields of worship. Forerunners were set apart for the Lord to cultivate hunger for the *suddenly* of God. There is now an unmistakable hunger for the Kingdom of Heaven to be established in the earth. We watch and wait with anticipation for the gates of revival to swing wide open.

Jesus said, in Luke 6:21:

Blessed (happy—with life joy and satisfaction in God's favor and salvation, apart from your outward condition—and to be envied) are you who hunger and seek with eager desire now, for you shall be filled and completely satisfied! Blessed (happy—with life-joy and satisfaction in God's favor and salvation, apart from your outward condition—and to be envied) are you who weep and sob now, for you shall laugh!

He who laughs last, laughs best; and He who sits in the Heavens and laughs will have the last laugh as the enemy is taken off guard at the Gate Beautiful (see Ps. 2:4). The very best wine was saved for last during the wedding at Cana (see John 2:1-11), and the very best wine of His habitation is reserved for the bridal shower revivals just prior to His glorious return; Hallelujah! In this chapter we will examine this Gideon army of Holy Ghost zealots and their role in ushering in a habitation of the Lord.

In January of 1994, the Lord brought renewal to the Church. We were refreshed in the Holy Spirit and renewed to our first love: Jesus. As the anointing of this move of the Lord spread around the world, it was both received and rejected. When the Holy Spirit moves, He will not be concerned with fitting into the acceptable mold of man's design. Frankly, if the *carnality* of man is not frustrated, then it is *not* the Holy Spirit that is manifesting. The Spirit and the flesh are at enmity with each other (see Gal. 5:17), but we are blessed in His presence when we live in the Spirit. In light of this, those who embraced the Holy Spirit's anointing openly were those with hearts like Gideon, which I will explain shortly. However, those who rejected the Holy Spirit were under the *influence* of a religious spirit, whose role is like the Midianites. *Midian* stands for "strife" and "contention,"[1] which is the nature of the religious spirit.

Judges describes the nature of the religious spirit:

For whenever Israel had sown their seed, the Midianites and the Amalekites and the people of the east came up against them. They would encamp against them and destroy the crops

*as far as Gaza and leave no nourishment for Israel, and no
ox or sheep or donkey* (Judges 6:3-4).

The Midianites and Amalekites came to destroy the sustenance of
Israel. God brought this judgment on Israel because they dis-
obeyed the command of the Lord by fearing the false gods of the
Amorites. Verse 5 says that they came "like locusts for multitude."
As we know, locusts destroy crops. The Midianites, like locusts,
came and destroyed the sustenance and fruit of Israel for seven
years. Like the Midianites, the religious spirit seeks to destroy the
sustenance, or the fruit, of the Church. It sought to bring strife
and contention when the Holy Spirit began to move among us
with signs and wonders, bringing expressive freedom and
metaphorically prophetic manifestations. Remember that we do
not wrestle against flesh and blood but against principalities and
powers (see Eph. 6:12). Those inclined toward the intellect and
those inclined toward the Holy Spirit were swiftly divided. Dis-
illusionment and disagreements were stirred up over the renewal.
Church splits ran rampant as the sword of the Lord divided the
soulish from the spiritual.

Why do you suppose God allowed all of this confusion?
Israel feared the false gods of the Amorites, and God judged that
idolatry for seven years through a Midianite assault on the harvest
of the land and livestock. Likewise, the Church has entertained
idolatry and a spirit of religion for many years. However, when
the renewal occurred, God used it to begin the process of repentance, and He began to reveal some of His strategies for revival.
Therefore, it was equally important for Him to bring judgment on
the false god of religion that His Church (like Israel) was flirting
with. Now you may ask, why would judgment on religion cause
God to allow the religious spirit (like Midian) to rise up against

the sustenance of the renewed Church? The answer is this: by letting this happen, God openly exposed the religious spirit, which was previously hidden and contentedly believing it was in control. When God brought the renewal, the religious spirit rose up with a fury against the Holy Spirit's anointing, in order to snuff out the fruit of new life. The Lord brought the refreshing rain of His Spirit, and His light shone in the darkness, revealing the sin within. This caused the religious spirit to spit venom in order to protect its throne, while making a spectacle of itself. The false god of religion has come out from behind the curtain and has become an easy target to spot. However, it's a target that only the Holy Ghost can hit; and He *will* abolish it through the worship and prayer of the Gideon army.

What is the Gideon Army? The Gideon Army is a name that I use to describe a remnant of radical, Spirit-led intercessors and prophetic worshipers who will operate in the anointing of the Holy Spirit in order to *tear down strongholds*, while seeking a holy *habitation* for the Lord. We are Holy Ghost zealots who can't conform to calculated, safe, man-pleasing methods.

My personal goal is to see the doors of religion blown off of the house of God through the anointing of the Holy Spirit upon radical, apostolic worship. I also want to see the Lord use this worship to destroy the doors of intellectualism that have blinded the lost in the streets. This is, in my opinion, the most important part of the restoration of the Tabernacle of David: to seek the Lord for a mercy seat on the town green where *all* can come into the presence of His glory. I am more excited about the "no veil" aspect of it than I am about the 24/7 aspect of it. The pews of predictability are ready to crumble at the sound of the Lord's trumpet, and we are getting ready to blow it loud and clear.

The Army of Gideon

I take the name for Gideon's Army from the story in Judges where God directs Gideon to prune his army down to only the men who lapped water when they drank:

So he brought the men down to the water, and the Lord said to Gideon, Everyone who laps up the water with his tongue as a dog laps it, you shall set by himself, likewise everyone who bows down on his knees to drink. And the number of those who lapped, putting their hand to their mouth, was 300 men, but all the rest of the people bowed down upon their knees to drink water. And the Lord said to Gideon, With the 300 men who lapped I will deliver you, and give the Midianites into your hand. Let all the others return every man to his home (Judges 7:5-7).

Like Gideon's remnant of 300 men, this worshiping army goes down to the river wearing the full armor of the Lord, wielding the sword of truth in one hand and lapping the water with the other. All faces look forward, and their unified gaze is fixed upon the Lord, poised for battle.

The Gideon Church is a united front. This little army of worship warriors is exclusively focused on revival, both regionally and worldwide, and is eager to *blow the trumpets* of the Lord and send the wicked stronghold of religion into confusion. There are yet many believers who will be snatched from the chains of religion to help reclaim the waterfords of the River Jordan, just as the Israelites did:

When [Gideon's men] blew the 300 trumpets, the Lord set every [Midianite's] sword against his comrade and against all the army, and the army fled as far as Beth-shittah toward Zererah, as far as the border of Abel-meholah by Tabbath. And the men of Israel were called together out of Naphtali and Asher and all Manasseh, and they pursued Midian. And Gideon sent messengers Through out all the hill country of Ephraim, saying, come down against the Midianites and take all the intervening fords as far as Beth-barah and also the Jordan. So all the men of Ephraim were gathered together and took all the fords as far as Beth-barah and also the Jordan (Judges 7:22-24).

As in this passage, the enemy will be blindsided and the spiritual Church of living stones will be released from religious oppression.

Many believers thirst for the *living* God and do not know that He is right at their finger tips, free for the asking. The institution of works-oriented Christianity, which puts good works into the methodology of salvation, is holding many true believers in deception. I hold onto the hope that all will come to repentance, abandon their dead works, and embrace the living God. You see, we all know that faith without works is dead (see James 2:14-26); however, works done out of religious duty are also dead (see Gal. 5:5-6). Works that are not fueled by God's love, compassion, directive, and *anointing* are an idol of the intellect, which makes the assent to human understanding the very model of man made religion.

I hate even mentioning these things, but I am compelled to give the whole truth without a sugar coating. Jesus taught us in the parable of the wheat and tares:

Let both grow together until the harvest: and in the time of harvest I will say to the reapers, 'Gather ye together first the tares, and bind them in bundles to burn them: but gather the wheat into my barn (Matthew 13:30 KJV).

The definition of the word *tares* is "false grain."[2] Also, Gideon's name means to "cut asunder and to hew down."[3] Now, I know that this Scripture calls forth heavenly angels at the close of the age. But I also believe that the Church will be involved in cooperation with Heaven's angels to reap a great harvest in the Day of the Lord. The Gideon Army battalions of the latter rain times are also the reapers. Verse 39 refers to the reapers as angels, but the definition of angels *in that particular verse* is "to bring tidings; a messenger, a drove-herd,"[4] or an army of messengers that I like to call the Army of Gideon. Thus, I believe that earthly angels (messengers) alongside heavenly angels will *cut asunder and hew down* the religious spirit, just like Gideon tore down the altars to Baal and Ashera in his day. Then they will gather together the last great harvest with the anointing of the Holy Spirit upon radical prophetic worship.

Multitudes of fiery worshipers gathered in the public courtyards, accompanied by Heaven's angels, will usher in God's river of life, and I project that whole cities will be won to the Lord in one grand sweep of His anointing. We are in the day of the harvest, which is why this truth is so powerful. This is not conjecture, this is revelation: "Now the Angel of the Lord came and sat under the oak (terebinth) at Ophrah, which belonged to Joash the Abiezrite, and his son Gideon was beating wheat in the winepress to hide it from the Midianites" (Judg. 6:11). When the Angel of the Lord visited Gideon, he was threshing wheat in the winepress to hide it from the Midianites. Threshing *wheat* is a symbol of the harvest; and in this particular scripture, I believe that threshing wheat in the *winepress* is a symbol of harvesting in the midst of an outpouring of the Holy Spirit. God often refers to the winepress as His indignation and wrath (see Rev. 14:19). However, He also uses wine as a symbol of His love and His presence (see Deut. 11:14, Prov. 3:10, Song of Sol. 7:9). The Lord was very *present* with Gideon in the winepress, and He gave Gideon instructions to take back the land for His glory. He saved the best wine for last in John 2:10, and He is saving the best wine for the last great harvest as well! As the harvest is gathered in this kind of winepress, new believers will be protected from the religious spirit under the umbrella of the Holy Spirit's anointing; just as Gideon protected his harvest of wheat from the Midianites.

Gideon was unsure of the validity of the Lord's visitation, so he asked Him if He would wait beneath the oak until he returned with an offering for Him.

> *Then Gideon went in and prepared a kid and unleavened cakes of an ephah of flour. The meat he put in a basket and the broth in a pot, and brought them to Him under the oak and presented them. And the Angel of God said to him, "Take the meat and unleavened cakes and lay them on this rock and pour the broth over them." And he did so. Then the Angel of the Lord reached out the tip of the staff that was in His hand, and touched the meat and the unleavened cakes, and there flared up fire from the rock and consumed the meat and the unleavened cakes. Then the Angel of the Lord vanished from his sight* (Judges 6:19-21).

The Lord instructed Gideon to place the entire offering on a nearby rock. The offering consisted of meat from a young female goat, unleavened cakes, and broth. Bear in mind that this offering was placed on the rock (which represents Jesus) and that fire came forth from the rock and consumed the whole sacrifice. Let me stretch you a little bit. I like to refer to the female goat as a prophetic picture of the Christian religious systems of today, which will be *destroyed* by the fire of God. Likewise, the unleavened cakes are a prophetic picture of the saints that get delivered from the religious spirit and are *refined* and *purified* in the fire of

God. Thus, they will lay their lives down prostrate upon the rock (Jesus), and His all-consuming fire will come forth as He is aroused with desire by such love-sick worship. Let us set ourselves ablaze, and let the world come to see us burn.

After the Lord accepted his offering, He returned later that evening to give Gideon these instructions:

> *That night the Lord said to Gideon, "Take your father's bull, the second bull seven years old, and pull down the altar of Baal that your father has, and cut down the Asherah [symbol of the goddess Asherah] that is beside it; And build an altar to the Lord your God on top of this stronghold with stones laid in proper order. Then take the second bull and offer a burnt sacrifice with the wood of the Asherah which you shall cut down"* (Judges 6:25-26).

Here Gideon was used by the Lord to tear down altars to false gods; thus his name means "to cut asunder and to hew down." Notice that the bull was seven years old. It was also the *second* bull. The word *second* in this particular scripture means to "alter, transmute, and to pervert."[5] What was perverted and transmuted here was the true spiritual worship of God. The *second* bull was *seven* years of age and represented the *seven* years that Israel suffered under Midianite oppression. I believe that it also symbolically prophesies the fullness of time when God will remove the influence of this bewitching religious spirit from His latter rain Church. Gideon presented this bull as a burnt offering in repentance for the sin of Israel's idolatry. Likewise, as the Church continues to repent, she is being delivered, little by little, day by day (individually and corporately), from the various forms of idolatry that hold her captive. This process has begun and shall continue throughout these last days until Christ's Church is fully reformed.

Gideon was commanded to tear down the altar to Baal and the Asherah, which was beside it, and to build in its place an altar to the Lord with stones laid in proper order. The stones laid in proper order prophesy about the *living stones* of our current day who will replace religion by building a proper altar to the Lord. This altar is a corporate ministry of perpetual spiritual worship and prayer—the restoration of the Tabernacle of David. This ministry of worship will have no ceiling to hold back the anointing, no fleshy politics, and no facades. The wood from the Asherah was used as fuel for the fire on the Lord's altar. Then the *second* bull, which represented spiritual perversion, was sacrificed and given as a burnt offering. I see the Asherah wood (which represents humanity) as a symbol of those who served religion for a time and then repented of their spiritual perversion to become fuel for the fire of God in pure, spiritual worship.

Shiloh Shall Emerge From the Eagle

I had a dream where I was in a gathering of worship warriors in a cave on a mountain, quite like David's group. Suddenly, an angel stood up to speak and said, "It's time for Shiloh!" All the warriors immediately left except me; I went to the angel to read from the book she was holding. Although I read a whole paragraph carefully, the Lord allowed me to remember only one phrase vividly, which was the very first sentence of the chapter. It said, "Shiloh shall emerge from the eagle." The Lord then showed me what this statement means. The eagle represents prophetic worshipers, and Shiloh is the presence of the Lord.[6] Thus, the presence of the Lord shall emerge from prophetic worship and intercession. Shiloh shall emerge from the eagle. My dear friend, Mimi Caban, who leads prophetic worship and intercession gatherings called Open Soaks, twice received the same prophecy from two different sources. The prophets both said, "I see your whole body covered with eagle feathers." So, you see, this metaphorical language of the Lord is a key to understanding our destiny.

When I awoke from this dream, I opened my Bible, and God immediately led me to this Scripture:

The scepter or leadership shall not depart from Judah, nor the ruler's staff from between his feet, until Shiloh [the Messiah, the Peaceful One] comes to Whom it belongs, and to Him shall be the obedience of the people (Genesis 49:10).

The King James Version puts it this way:

The scepter shall not depart from Judah, nor a lawgiver from between his feet, until Shiloh come; and unto Him shall the gathering of the people be (Genesis 49:10 KJV).

The scepter shall be with Judah. *Judah* means "to revere or worship with extended hands, and to make confession, praise, and thanksgiving."[7] The Lord dwells in Judah. Psalm 114:2 says that "Judah became [God's] sanctuary (the Holy Place of His *habitation*), and Israel His dominion." Similarly, Psalm 76:1–2 says, "In Judah God is known *and* renowned; His name is highly praised *and* is great in Israel. In [Jeru]Salem also is His tabernacle, and His dwelling place is in Zion." The Lord dwells in the worship of His people. Since He inhabits worship, it is guaranteed that He will emerge from that place of habitation, the praises of His people. The Army of Gideon will become a living sacrificial fuel for His fire. Let the worshipers and intercessors arise to form the Lord's army of spiritual worship and prayer.

Quicken us, Lord, to perpetrate Your will in the land for the glory of Your Holy Name. Your scepter and authority have been and shall be with Judah (praise) until You come. As we declare Your name and Your heart before a dying world, emerge with

Your awesome presence, and flood the whole earth with Your glorious light. Truly, the people will be gathered unto You, for when You are lifted up, You shall draw all men unto Yourself!

CHAPTER 5

A Storm Named Mercy

Mercy triumphs over judgment (see James 2:13). Mercy is the most costly gift in the universe, and God's unyielding determination to bestow mercy on sinners is awesome to the point of great, fearful reverence. God's mercy makes Heaven's sinless angels shudder with reverence and awe. Truly, reverent fear is due to the God whose hands hold the future of all that lives. If a man was to meet the living God while in a state of uncleansed sin, the perfect holiness of God and His incredible mercy would likely cause the man to shrink away with cringing fear. But Jesus didn't shed one drop of blood in vain. The Lord begins to show mercy and passionate desire for this man, wooing him, courting him into the revelation of his first love, Jesus. The man has just found himself facing the Door of forgiveness, the Gate of mercy, the Lord of the gospel of grace, his lover, Jesus. Is it possible for someone to reject such love? Could self condemnation be so strong that it thwarts the outstretched arms of Jesus? It is not the Lord's desire that any should perish, but that all inherit eternal life (see 2 Peter 3:9)

A love revival is coming and mercy is the theme. This will not be a revival that wins the intellect of men to a belief system of religion. This will be a revival that wins the hearts of sinners to a living God whose mercy is revealed in His manifested presence. The Lord is restoring the revelation of His gospel of grace to every believer, and we will be the hands, the feet, and the voice of the Lord (His Body), that brings this *tangible* message to His harvest. Let the tidal wave of His love be poured out upon these last few generations of natural history, and let the fires of love unite His finished and perfected Bride. Amen and Amen!

We are ever so close to a mighty move of God. We've been praying for the Lord to send the rain of His Spirit to the cities of the world, and the manifestation of our hearts' desire is beginning to unfold all around us. When He sends His rain, a flood of the knowledge of the glory of the Lord will fill the earth as the waters cover the sea (see Hab. 2:14). If you are not prepared for this cataclysmic event, this wave of glory might very well knock you over. We should all endeavor to be prepared, like one of the *wise* virgins (see Matt. 25:1-13). But how can we prepare for something that will come suddenly, without warning? Make up your mind to go with God. You *know* the times that we are in. Become someone who decides to seek the Lord for the fulfillment of His desires, and you *will* be prepared with the anointing oil of intercession, even if you stay in your prayer closet. Anna interceded all of her life before Jesus came. I am convinced that we won't have to wait until we are in Heaven to see many of the glories that I will yet describe in this book.

We all know what happens when people on a coastline are warned about a hurricane and they pay no attention to the warning. A very calculated storm comes and consumes them mercilessly. The storm of God's glory is not calculated by men, so we have only the Holy Spirit as our barometer. Thank God for that. Fortunately for us, the Lord is coming with a storm named Mercy rather than Ivan the Terrible. Yet this is the great and terrible day of the Lord (see Joel 2:11). We want to be prepared like giant eagles that are mounted up and ready for the winds, like Gideon eagles that lap the water with one talon, gird their wings for the high places, and keep their eagle eyes fixed on the lightnings of God.

The Dream

The Lord sent a dream to me where I was standing on the shore of the ocean. The ocean itself was empty, but a giant wave came that was about three hundred feet tall. I had no fear at all as this wave came. I dove straight into it, and it carried me along without any struggle right up to the top. I didn't have to do anything; I didn't even have to swim. I just rode upon this wave as if protected in its bosom. As I was floating along on the top of the wave, I was very aware that this represented the wave of the Holy Spirit flooding the earth. It was a thing of beauty. But all of a sudden, it also became alarmingly clear to me that everything below me and under the water was dead. Then the Lord brought me to this Scripture:

> *For in seven days I will cause it to rain upon the earth forty days and forty nights, and every living substance and thing that I have made I will destroy, blot out, and wipe away from the face of the earth* (Genesis 7:4).

I thought that was rather peculiar, wondering, "Why would the Lord bring me to that Scripture?" Then the Lord gave me revelation, which I penned as fast as possible. This is what He said:

> The seven days represent the seven millennial days of human history. The world has just entered the dawn of

that seventh day, the end of the age. As I sent the natural rain in the days of Noah, so shall I send the rain of the Spirit in the seventh day at the end of the age. Those who belong to My Kingdom are not of this world but are citizens of Heaven. All who are called by My name, but are yet to enter in, will indeed enter in during these days. Even as the floodwaters purged from the depths, so shall rivers of living waters burst forth with revival through My people. I will send my River of delights when worshipers gather in spirit and in truth. I will release a sound from Heaven through My people, and they will be holy gates in the public meeting place, and all who are called by My name will receive salvation through My Son, Jesus. However, those who will not come to the beckoning call of the Holy Spirit will be crushed, for the worship of the Lord is a snare to His enemies. My word says, "And whoever falls on this Stone will be broken to pieces, but he on whom It falls will be crushed to powder [and It will winnow him, scattering him like dust]" (Matt. 21:44). However, the worship of the Lord will be as a chariot for those who are to inherit eternal life. Selah.

A flood of glory is coming, and those who bear the ark of the Lord and worship Him in spirit and in truth will float freely upon the waters of life. Noah's ark is a type of the latter rain Church, bearing the ark of the Lord and riding upon the floodwaters of the Holy Spirit. Those who bear the ark of the Lord in these times are His worshipers (His holy gates), through whom the King of Glory will come in (see Ps. 24:7) and through whom the crowds of pilgrims from all nations shall enter (see Ps. 87:2). In these times, the times of the restoration of all things, the saving knowledge of Christ will be made known all over the world through the restoration of true spiritual and prophetic worship, as the Lord perfects the praises of His people. He will shape, form, and make perfect the story of His wonderful cross.

In answer to the religious leaders of His day, who were critical of the ways that the children were praising God, Jesus said "Yea; have ye never read, 'out of the mouth of babes and sucklings thou hast perfected praise'" (Matt. 21:16b KJV). When the Lord said, "Out of the mouth of babes and sucklings, thou hast perfected praise," He spoke of the simple-minded, or childlike in faith.[1] Through this childlike, yielded Bride, He shall perfect praise. The word *praise* in this Scripture literally means "story;" the story of the Lord made perfect within the context of song and high exaltation.[2] Thus, praise and worship will operate with the Spirit of prophecy, and will be given keen articulation as the song of the Lord comes forth.

The Lord is focused on His people coming into the full knowledge of Him in these days. The kind of worship that we are going to experience in the days ahead requires a much greater revelation of Jesus. We can only worship the Lord according to the revelation of Him that we have. Imagine if we have never had the experience of the infilling of the Holy Spirit. Our worship would be reduced to a mere expression of the carnal understanding of Scripture, and it would also be limited by how we received the word from the evangelist. Further, we would be subject to every word of the preacher without having our own heavenly guide into all truth (see John 16:13). What a terrible thought! Thank God we have been given the Holy Spirit and have experiential knowledge of Christ. Of course, God would have it no other way. He is ready to pour out more and more revelation upon His Church. He intends for us to enter into realms of worship that are much higher and deeper. We will taste and see how beloved we are to Him.

Brace yourself for visitations that will develop a foundation for true fervency fueled by the joy of the Lord. The joy of His salvation and the joy of His very person will be our strength (see Neh. 8:10). Brace yourself for a storm named Mercy that will leave you breathless. A wave of the frightful mercy of God is coming and the world will not know what landed on shore. Those who are prepared to ride this glorious wave of the Holy Spirit will lack nothing they need for the days ahead. They will lack nothing because they will have a greater revelation of Jesus than they have ever had before. They will know what Paul meant when he said, "I can do all things through Christ who strengthens me" (see Phil. 4:13).

CHAPTER 6

Worship and the Word

One of the most relevant factors concerning the renewal is that after experiencing the movement of the Holy Spirit, several Scriptures have taken on more life. Once again, greater revelation of the Lord has been poured out upon us, resulting in greater fathoms of experience in worship. Through the renewal, we have been prepared for the next wave of glory that we discussed in the previous chapter. The Church was in a famine of revelation for quite some time, so it is understandable that we would be fed revelation little by little. You don't eat a full course meal complete with fillet mignon after a forty-day water fast. Likewise, it would not have been beneficial to be force-fed too much revelation after spending a long season in a spiritual wilderness. My personal favorite part of the renewal is how the word of God has just opened up in fresh and powerful ways. Being a worship leader *as well* as a preacher, this has given me lots of fuel to burn. In this chapter, we will take a brief look at some of the Scriptures that validate our experience with the Lord. It seems that we have already done a lot of that already, but this chapter is directly geared toward that end. I have never read a book that covered this kind of material, so I am highly honored to share this with you.

Psalm 9:14 says, "...I will *rejoice* in thy salvation" (KJV). The translators chose to use the word *rejoice* in this Scripture for the Hebrew word *guwl*, which means to "spin round under the influence of any *violent* emotion."[1] Consider the key word—*violent*—in the definition of *guwl*. The definition of *violent* is "marked by extreme force or a sudden intense activity; extremely excited."[2] This scripture takes on a far more lively description when the term *violent* is included in the translation. When studying a passage, I like to use the literal Hebrew or Greek definition as given in the *Strong's Exhaustive Concordance of the Bible*. I then take key English words from that definition and expound upon their meanings as well. This enables me to create as true a translation as can be expected from our pale English language. Often a phrase would better translate the meaning of a verse rather than a solitary English word. Such is the case in this Scripture. In my opinion, the solitary word *rejoice* simply doesn't cut it.

The world has a universal definition of violence as it relates to anger and physical abuse; however, the Lord uses the word violent in reference to worship and rejoicing. Consider the above literal definition of the Hebrew word guwl and compare it to the word *rejoice*. *Rejoice* means "to feel joy or great delight."[3] This word rejoice is only telling half of the story. If I translated a Bible version of this verse, I would have used the following phrase (instead of the word *rejoice*) in order to capture the meaning of the Hebrew word guwl: "I will spin around with violent, radical joy as I muse upon the reality of God's salvation for me."

In Matthew 11:12, Jesus said, "...The kingdom of heaven suffereth violence, and the violent take it by force" (KJV). These words, *violence* and *violent*, describe those who have been violated by the enemy or have had things that are rightfully theirs seized by the enemy. If you have been a victim of this injustice, you now have the authority to take back with violence that which you have suffered from the kingdom of darkness.[4] It's my opinion that the Lord's most radical and violent acts against darkness are His unmerited favor, His everlasting and unconditional love, and His eternal and tender mercies toward His redeemed. I also think that the most damaging blow that we can blacken the enemy's eye with is to worship the Lord in the beauty of holiness, declaring His goodness, majesty, and grace, and most of all, to declare His mercy that endures forever.

Who would have thought that joy, rejoicing, and something we "river folks" like to call holy laughter would have such an enormous effect of violence against the devil? God did! Psalm 149:1 says, "Praise the Lord! Sing to the Lord a new song, *And* His praise in the assembly of saints" (NKJV). This word *praise* is from the Hebrew word *halal*, which means "to shine…make a show… be (clamorously) foolish; to rave…celebrate…feign mad…[and rage]."[5] Notice how this is different from the meaning of the word *praise* in Matthew 21:16, which I mentioned in Chapter 5. In fact, there are seventeen different definitions of the word *praise* in Scripture; many will happen concurrently during spiritual worship. Psalm 149:5 says, "Let the saints be joyful in glory: let them sing aloud upon their beds" (KJV). The word *sing* in this scripture is from the Hebrew word *ranan*, which means "to creak or (emit stridulous sound)."[6] Tell me, what kind of worship is marked by clamorously foolish behavior? Isn't making a show the same thing as a performance? To shine is understandable, but to rage? One of the meanings of *rage* is "an intense feeling; passion." Another is "a fit of violent wrath."[7] Now that seems to go along with what we were just discussing a bit earlier, doesn't it? So, what kind of worship is marked by *all* these things? It is the kind of worship that God intends for us to enter into.

The Lord inhabits Judah (the praises of His saints). In Isaiah 30:31-32 it says that He smites His enemies with His rod, to the sound of timbrels and lyres. Also, Psalms 110:2 states, "The Lord shall send the *rod* of thy strength out of Zion: rule thou in the midst of thine enemies" (KJV). We are the rod, branch, or tribe,[8] and He sends us forth from Zion with worship to smite the enemy. Similarly, Joel 3:16 says, "The Lord will thunder and roar from Zion and utter His voice from Jerusalem, and the heavens and the earth shall shake; but the Lord will be a refuge for His people and a stronghold to the children of Israel." The Lord also shall *roar* out of Zion. We *are* Zion my friends. I have personally seen the manifestation of roaring come forth in intercession as an act of judgment against demonic strongholds. I have also seen roaring come forth to *make a show* of the enemy and to exalt the Lion of Judah during highly anointed times of worship. There's that phrase *make a show* again. So go ahead, make a show, be foolish for Christ, celebrate, and emit stridulous sound. Declare God's truth in song. Shine, and in your shining, let the Lord have His violent wrath against darkness as He inhabits Judah (the praises of His people).

I could go on and on; however I'll wrap it up with this last example from Ezekiel's vision of Heaven. "And above the firmament that was over their heads was the likeness of a throne in appearance like a sapphire stone, and seated above the likeness of a throne was a likeness with the appearance of a Man" (Ezek. 1:26). The throne of sapphires that the Lord rests upon here is the worship of His redeemed. Sapphires are a foundational stone of the New Jerusalem and represent "celebration: to show forth, to make a tally, commune, and to declare."[9] *Commune* means "to administer or receive communion, and to communicate intimately."[10] All of the above meanings of sapphire point to worship. Song of Solomon 5:14 describes the Body of Christ: "...His *body* is a figure of bright ivory overlaid with [*veins of*] *sapphires.*" In the King James Version, the word *belly* is used; in the Amplified, the word *body* is used. In this passage, the word *belly* is not only defined as the stomach area but also as the womb.[11] *We* are His Body, and our spiritual womb has been impregnated to birth the lost into His Kingdom. Bright ivory represents sanctified flesh, and His people who are sanctified and washed in the blood of Jesus have *veins of sapphires* (spiritual worship). This worship of the Lord *is* the vein that carries His blood to every member of His Body. His blood, carried in the veins of spiritual worship, will flow to all of His Body and to all of those who are called by His holy name for healing and salvation.

In Rick Joyner's book *The Final Quest*, Rick describes a panoramic vision of Heaven, in which he receives a teaching from a prophetic being in the form of an eagle. The eagle says:

> True worship also pours the precious oil upon the head, Jesus, which then flows down over the entire body making us one with Him and with each other. No one who comes into union with Him will remain wounded or unclean. His blood is pure life, and it flows when we are joined to Him. When we are joined to Him we are also joined to the rest of the body so that His blood flows through all. Is that not how you heal a wound to your body, by closing the wound so that the blood can flow to the wounded member to bring regeneration? When a

part of His body is wounded, we must join in unity with
that part until it is fully restored. We are all one.[12]

So you see, when we corporately offer *true* spiritual worship to
the Lord in unity, the oil is poured upon His head. We become
one with Him and with each other. Through this spiritual worship, we come into union with Him and with the rest of His Body
so that His blood flows through all the members. Isn't this a wonderful confirmation of Song of Solomon 5:14? This truly paints a
picture of how worship will be used by the Lord to stir up a great
revival. The more radical and offensive worship becomes to the
carnal mind, the closer to a revival outbreak we will be. If you
don't believe me, remember this: the things of the Spirit are offensive to the flesh. The natural man and the Spirit have nothing in
common unless the natural man is fully submitted to the control
of the Holy Spirit. So hop on the bus; God's on the move!

CHAPTER 7

Rainmaker, Hosanna

Global is a word that comes to mind when we speak of the latter rain revivals. The first nation fathers of all the lands have a specific, God-ordained authority as they receive the Lord to bless the land and call forth the inheritance of the Lord. It is no wonder that the Lord called forth the indigenous people during the Toronto meetings. God is up to a very large-scale gathering of the Bride. We tend to be focused on our own corner of the world, but this is a big planet with many cultures and peoples. Our God desires to bring them *all* under one open Heaven and to have them *all* fly one flag of universal liberty.

There were forerunners to the Toronto blessing and there are now forerunners to the next move of God. He is bringing us ever closer to the greatest awakening that this world has ever seen. The forerunners that have now been set apart for the Lord are posted strategically on the four corners of the earth. Even if they are unaware of how the Lord is using them, they are indeed being used to oil the land with the flammable anointing of the Holy Spirit. We will see just how pivotal the Toronto blessing was in the scheme of the Lord to hasten His Great Day. The effects are still snowballing to this day. If ever there was a reason to teach the butterfly effect from a heavenly viewpoint, what God started in Toronto certainly qualifies.

My wife, Judith, received a revelation from the Lord in 1991, before she met me, concerning the rain of the Spirit that was coming. God would touch the Church all over the world with a very fresh and intimate move of His Spirit, bringing renewal to the Church with the illumination and revelation of the Son of God. For twelve years previous to this, Judith and a core group of her friends were experiencing an intimate touch of the Holy Spirit and the new wine of renewal accompanied by manifestations. All this happened prior to the Toronto Blessing. They couldn't have been the only people experiencing this. There must have been others all over the world, small pockets of people experiencing this touch and being used of the Lord as forerunners to intercede for this move of the Holy Spirit that would ultimately touch the worldwide Church.

These forerunners were intercessors like Anna of the temple (see Luke 2:36-38), with a slight twist. Their intercession took place in their prayer caves rather than in the meeting place of the Church, in order to preserve them from the persecution of the religious spirit which was dominant in the Church at that time. The Church at large was dressed with appearances, expressing Christian beliefs behind a veil of hidden agendas and vanity. To this day, the Lord is still pruning the Church of these things. These appearances and facades have been the very thing that has kept the world from expressing any interest in what we have in Christ. The world doesn't want religious appearances. They want the real deal. They want a Holy Spirit-filled Church that manifests the reality and power of Jesus Christ like the *true* Pentecostal Church in the book of Acts, those "drunken" folks in the upper room. They were *not* drunk on alcohol as was supposed. Rather, they were drunk on the Holy Spirit and a fresh outpouring of *power* from on high (see Acts 2:1-40).

Now consider this: for the crowds to say that they were drunk implies that the upper room gang must have appeared drunk and were obviously manifesting in a way that was offensive to the carnal understanding of the crowd. But then the "drunkards" began to preach, and the anointing of the Holy Ghost fell, and three thousand were saved! Can you imagine what *three thousand* drunks looked like? Perhaps it was a little bit like Toronto. In the same way, the crowds at Toronto were not drunk on alcohol, as may have been supposed. Nevertheless, people were staggering into hotel lobbies at 1:00 AM or later, and others were being carried in from the street. We were touched by the hand of God, and the human response to this touch looked rather bizarre. I believe this bizarre array of Holy Spirit shenanigans was the plan of God to confound those who were wise in their own eyes. Some of these manifestations were prophetic demonstrations that declared, in part, the future move of God, but they also showed forth His knowledge and sovereignty over our personal circumstances. It was as if the Lord decided to play a spiritual game of charades with us.

Also, some of these symbolically prophetic manifestations were calling forth indigenous peoples. Judith and I went to the world gathering of Christian indigenous peoples in South Dakota in the fall of 1998. It was beautiful to see the indigenous (first nations) people from many different nations gathered together to praise and worship God. Every nation that was represented expressed their Christianity and their worship of the Lord through a variety of diverse cultural traditions, songs, and dances. Don't confuse the word *tradition* with religion. All cultures have traditions, but the religious spirit is a Church-wide cancer. Religion is an institutionalized system of religious attitudes, a system of beliefs designed by men to cater to their quasi-legalistic fear of basic spiritual truths. But in many cases, cultural tradition is something that distinguishes one people group from another, like a beauty mark.

Many nations and denominations were represented at this gathering of Christian indigenous peoples. This was the first fruits of spiritual Israel coming together as one and embracing one another in love. They embraced a spirit of repentance for the wrongful things done to one another, and they embraced and accepted one another as valid, honorable Christian people. I was on cloud nine the entire ten days that I was there. It was like watching a fetus being conceived in the womb, knowing that the baby would be born very soon. Their presentations consisted of war cries and chants, drums and all forms of music, various styles of dress, and a variety of dances and symbolic expressions that are deeply woven into the fabric of their cultural roots. These artfully expressive forms of communication are all a part of who they are as a people. They were doing these things to declare the gospel of Christ and as an expression of worship unto Christ.

Interestingly, three years earlier in Toronto we had heard and seen some of the same sounds and bodily manifestations produced prophetically by the Holy Spirit. Judith and I believe that many of the prophetic manifestations that occurred at Toronto through common North American mongrels (like ourselves) were calling forth the indigenous peoples and the nations. But we didn't get that revelation until we saw the indigenous peoples perform the *exact same* manifestations in the *natural* at South Dakota three years later. They were performing very natural acts of their own cultures that go back as far as their earliest forefathers.

Concerning the nations, Jeremiah 12:15 says, "And after I have plucked them up, I will return and have compassion on them and will bring them back again, every man to his heritage and every man to his land." He will restore the nations and the heritage of the nations. The diverse nations are coming together under one open Heaven to embrace one another in the love of Christ. Clearly, what happened in the renewal was the *real deal*, and the lost will only respond to the *real deal*.

Back in 1991, the Lord gave Judith a very clear and accurate revelation of what would soon transpire in Toronto. To accompany this revelation, He gave her a song, which she titled "Rainmaker." There is a short, but *key* chorus to that song which is comprised of these two words: "Rainmaker, hosanna." When renewal broke out in Toronto, the Lord sent the refreshing rain of His Spirit (a gentle sprinkle compared to what is soon coming). This renewal brought a fresh revelation of Jesus to His people, causing us to look into the mirror, remember who we are, and return to our first love. Acts 3:19 says, "Repent ye therefore, and be converted, that your sins might be blotted out, when the *times of refreshing* shall come from the presence of the Lord" (KJV). We call it renewal because we were renewed in our relationship with the Lord Jesus. We were renewed and refreshed in the presence of His Holy Spirit. This prepared us very well for the time when the *hosanna* part of the song would come to pass. *Hosanna* means "O save"[1] and "having salvation."[2] It refers to the harvest that would come after the renewal. This is found in the next verse of the Acts 3 passage: "And He shall send Jesus Christ, which before was preached unto you" (Acts 3:20 KJV).

Jesus Christ is going to visit His Church all over the world with signs, wonders, and resurrection power. The Church has been in a state of reformation and spiritual preparation for the

Day of the Lord: the *seventh* day from Adam and the *third* day from Jesus' first coming. The number *seven* represents perfection and the word *perfection* is defined as "flawlessness, saintliness, and an exemplification of supreme excellence."[3] The Church, of course, will reflect this perfection according to the Word of God when He returns. The Bible says that *all things* will be reconciled back to God (see Col. 1:20). Revelation 10:7 says, "…God's mystery (His secret design, His hidden purpose)… should be fulfilled (accomplished, completed)." The fully reformed Church, both Jew and Gentile, will discover these mysteries and see the fulfillment of God's purposes. The Lord is shaking and sifting the denominations as He prepares us for seasons of great harvest. Soon the Church of Christ will be recognized as the spiritual nation of Israel, rather than as a conglomerate of dysfunctional religious organizations. As prophets, priests, and kings, we shall reign on the earth as God originally intended from the first millennium.

> Your people cry, Hosanna!
> Glory to God in the highest!
> Blessed is He Who comes
> in the name of the Lord!
> Hosanna in the highest!
> All heaven and earth declare
> the glory of our risen King!
> Hosanna in the highest!
> The splendor of His majesty
> is brighter than ten thousand
> noon day suns! Hosanna in the
> highest! Who can compare to
> the glory of the Lord?
> Every tribe and every tongue
> will confess His Lordship.

Rainmaker, Hosanna

Every knee will bow.
Hosanna in the highest!
There is only one salvation
and only one Lord through
Whom it comes. Our God is
One! Hosanna in the highest!

CHAPTER 8

Landmarks of Redemptive History

S piritual landmarks have been established through very specific events and people over the last six thousand years, and they are found sequentially in approximately one thousand-year increments. These events are not separated by exact one thousand-year folders. Each millennium is as a day to the Lord, which I will cover with Scripture soon. In the back of the book, I have included a chart which shows the actual calendar of events chronologically. These landmarks serve as a scale in the Lord's map of redemptive history. To start, I will dedicate the beginning of this extensive chapter to exploring the role that Adam and Eve played in the plan of God to establish His counterpart Bride. So please forgive me if this seems like a bunny trail. After all, had it not been for these facts concerning Adam and Eve, there would be no Bride of Christ to write a book about in the first place.

The function of this chapter is to describe the spiritual landmarks that map out the intentions of the Lord's heart to bring about the fullness of time. Since the landmarks commence with Adam and Eve, I will begin there and then cover the proceeding landmarks, such as Noah, Abraham, David, Jesus, the dark ages, etcetera, and finally this very day in which we now live. It is important to take a look at the road map to glory as planned by the Lord through the millenniums. Without history, there would be no story to begin with. After all, we are really talking about His-Story, and not history as we normally think of it.

God knew that Adam and Eve would fall in the time of temptation, just as He knew that lucifer would rebel. However, the Lord did not create evil. Scripture makes it abundantly clear that God is Light and that in Him there is no darkness at all (see 1 John 1:5). In James 1:13 it says that God tempts no one; therefore, satan's rebellion was of his own accord. The source for evil is found in the *untempted* choice of lucifer to rebel against God. Speaking of lucifer, Ezekiel says:

> *You were in Eden, the garden of God; every precious stone was your covering, the carnelian, topaz, jasper, chrysolite, beryl, onyx, sapphire, carbuncle, and emerald; and your settings and your sockets and engravings were wrought in gold. On the day that you were created they were prepared. You were the anointed cherub that covers with overshadowing [wings], and I set you so. You were upon the holy mountain of God; you walked up and down in the midst of the stones of fire [like the paved work of gleaming sapphire stone upon which the God of Israel walked on Mount Sinai]. You were blameless in your ways from the day you were created until iniquity and guilt were found in you* (Ezekiel 28:13-15).

In this scripture, lucifer is described as being blameless in his ways from the day that he was created *until* iniquity and guilt were found in him. He was the anointed cherub and was a beautiful being (righteous and holy), *before* he rebelled. But the Lord

God, in all of His wisdom, knew that he would indeed rebel. He used lucifer's rebellion to test Adam and Eve. This was mankind's first encounter with evil.

God allowed the natural course of things to take their shape. He didn't stand in the way; rather, He presided over the events. Our sovereign God had a divine plan in mind. In its application, He allowed human beings to have their first experience with *temptation*, and their first experience of having their freedom of choice tested. He gave us the free will to choose between righteousness and evil. But, if evil had not arrived on the scene *through* satan, we would not have had the circumstance to exercise that freedom of choice, to *choose* to either love God or own carnal passions. This is very critical, because the Lord God who desires a Bride must have a Bride who *chooses* Him freely, just as *He chose* us in Christ from before the foundations of the world (see Eph. 1:4).

In Genesis 3:22, God says of Adam after he had eaten the fruit, "Behold, the man has *become like* one of us." This implies that we were previously *not like* Him. Marital love demands two specific conditions: first, the bride and groom must be compatible or *like* one another; second, the bride and groom must *choose* one another. God already chose us; however, we were not able to choose God until the fall, which made it not only possible to choose Him, but also imperative to do so. If Adam and Eve had not fallen into temptation, they would have left humanity in a condition without the knowledge of good and evil. Genesis 3:22 would never have been written. Jesus would never have become our Savior, because we wouldn't have needed Him to be. And a spousal relationship with Jesus would not be an option. This is all very fragile, you see. Judith asked the Lord, "Why did You *allow* evil?" He answered, "I wanted to be your Savior and Husband!"

My friends, if that doesn't sum it up, nothing will. God used the fall of His first two loved ones to set the precedent for the rest of mankind, giving us the option to choose Him. Our Lover wasted no time!

So, this almost sounds like I am saying that God set them up for the fall, doesn't it? But He can't be accused of that since He created them with a *free will* and a carnal nature. The fall was inevitable; it was only a matter of time. He didn't create demi-gods; He created children that would have to *choose* Him and *grow* into His likeness. Truly, God did not make a mistake that He had to fix with the cross of Christ. The Lord knew full and well how His plan to create a counterpart Bride would unfold throughout the millenniums. He was aware of His cross before creation began! If it were not for the fall of Adam and Eve, there would be no Bride of Christ, there would be no Savior or Husband, and we would never have been able to *consummate* a Spirit to spirit marital relationship with the Lord.

After the Lord created, He said, "it is good," and it was. However, they (Adam and Eve) were not in a position to swoon after their Creator like lovers. They were children, created in His image; they were good, but not finished. After each day of creation, He said it was good, but he did not say He was finished. He didn't say *"it is finished"* until He breathed His last on the cross (see John 19:30). Since that day, we who choose Him are being perfected in the Spirit, going from glory to glory. As Paul wrote:

> And all of us, as with unveiled face, [because we] continued to behold [in the word of God] as in a mirror the glory of the Lord, are constantly being transfigured into His very own image in ever increasing splendor and from one degree of

glory to another; [for this comes] from the Lord [Who is] the Spirit (2 Corinthians 3:18).

We are not being restored to the former glory that the *first* Adam had before the fall; after all, this would be transgressing and not progressing. They were unfit for marriage with the Lord at that time. Rather, we are being transfigured into the perfect likeness of Christ, the second Adam and our *Husband* to be!

Adam and Eve were created during the sixth day, then God rested from His work, and they lived in the *seventh* day, the day of God's rest. Now, Adam existed for a period of time before Eve was formed from his rib. We do not have knowledge of how long a period of time this was; we only know that Eve was God's final work on the sixth day (see Gen. 1:26-31). Adam and Eve entered into the Lord's Day of rest, and then shortly thereafter, they fell. Therefore, the *seventh* day of the Lord's rest and the first day of man's fallen state overlap. The Bible says, when Adam had lived 130 years, that he had a son in his own likeness, in his own image, and he named him Seth (see Gen. 5:3). Then after Seth was born, Adam lived 800 years and had other sons and daughters. Altogether Adam lived 930 years and then he died. So this is the *first day* of fallen man. The *seventh* day, the day of God's rest, over-lapped with the first day of fallen man. In the same way, the *last* day of fallen man that we are now embarking upon will overlap with the day of God's rest (the *seventh* day), and the first day of kingdom life with the Lord (the millennial reign).

More Landmarks

Adam and Eve set the stage for the seven thousand-year period of human history as we know it; of these, we have now recorded six. These millennial periods are considered as days unto the Lord, and are approximately one thousand-year periods.

As Peter wrote, "...*With the Lord one day is as a thousand years and a thousand years as one day*" (2 Pet. 3:8).

After Adam died, the first day of fallen man had been recorded, and the second began with the life of Noah as the landmark. Noah was the only righteous man on the earth in his day; so God commanded him to build the ark which would float freely atop the flood waters that would consume the earth. The Lord told him,

> In **seven** days I will cause it to rain; so go into the ark, you and your whole family, for I have found you to be righteous in this generation. Take with you **seven** pairs of every kind of clean animal, and **seven** pairs of every kind of clean bird, for in **seven** days I will send the rain (Genesis 7:1–4, my paraphrase).

I see Noah's ark as a type of Christ and the latter rain Church. The ark would carry righteous Noah and his family upon the flood waters, and in it they would gather together the remnant of all clean animals and birds. I am not trying to make this a doctrine; however, it's truly interesting that the Church is now that vessel of righteousness which will ride upon the flood waters of the Holy Spirit and gather together for Christ "*the remnant of Edom and of all the nations*" (see Amos 9:11-12). Jesus even said that "[just] *as it was in the days of Noah, so will it be in the time of the Son of man*" (Luke 17:26).

Here are just a few of the parallels that I see between the story of Noah and the coming events of the Day of the Lord. It's simply interesting that Noah's flood was forecasted in chapter *seven* of Genesis, since after telling Noah, God brought the rain within *seven* natural days to flood the earth; The parallel is: God will bring the rain of the Spirit in the *seventh* millennial day to flood the earth (see Hosea 6:3, Hab. 2:14). *Seven* pairs of every kind of clean animal were gathered into the ark; and the remnant of all nations on *seven* continents will be gathered to the ark (Jesus). The Lord replenished the earth after the flood of Noah; and the new heavens and new earth will be presented after the millennial reign (see Rev. 21:1-3). These examples are just the tip of the iceberg when it comes to biblical synonyms. A library of them could be researched, I'm sure.

After the second millennial day, Noah died, and the third day began as Abraham became the father of our faith while receiving the promise of the New Covenant. He foreshadowed the cross of Christ by offering his only son Isaac as a sacrifice on Mount Moriah. It seems appropriate that the first mention of the word *worship* in the Bible is found in Genesis 22:5, which describes Abraham laying his only son, Isaac, upon an altar to God as a sacrifice.

At the end of the third millennial day and the beginning of the fourth, King David brought the ark of the Lord to the city of David. He established an earthly model or shadow of throne-room worship in the earth, and he showed forth a picture of the latter rain Church as a royal priesthood who would worship in spirit and in truth. David's ministry was a shadow of our universal priestly ministry unto the Lord. David was a prophet, priest, and king: a type of Jesus. Jesus, of course, is not only a prophet, but literally God's living word, our High Priest according to the order of Melchizedek (see Heb. 6:20), and the King of kings who will sit on David's throne.

At the end of the fourth millennial day and the beginning of the fifth, Jesus was born in fulfillment of the Scriptures. He came bearing the fullness of God within Him. He became the perfect fulfillment of the law, establishing the age of grace and salvation through His death and resurrection.

At the end of the fifth millennial day and the beginning of the sixth, there was a great religious war between Islam and Christianity over Jerusalem and the Holy Land. Partway through the sixth day and the dark ages, Martin Luther appeared on the scene and the *reformation* of the Church began. Now we are at the culmination of the sixth millennial day. The world is in an uproar, and something incredibly powerful is about to take place. We are at the end of the sixth millennial day and are truly bridging the *seventh*. The thief on the cross who cried out to Jesus for salvation bridged the gap between the age of the Law and the age of grace (see Luke 23:42-43). He lifted up a clarion call to the world, defining *those end-times*, by declaring Christ as *coming into His Kingdom*. Truly, Christ came into His kingdom when He ascended to Heaven and was presented to the Father (Acts 1:9-11, Dan. 7:13-14). Imagine the joy of that thief when Jesus remembered him. Likewise, we bridge the gap between the Church age of natural history and the age of the millennial reign to come. The seventh day from Adam is the same as the third day from Christ. There have been six millennial days since the fall of Adam and Eve, and the seventh is just around the corner. Likewise, there have been two millennial days since the time of Christ, and we are just at the crux of the third. Jesus referred to this day when He said, "…And the third day I shall be perfected" (Luke 13:32 KJV).

Let's do a brief *third day* study so that we can tie together the third day and the seventh day, leaving out any room for confusion. In the story of Abraham, Isaac was a type of Jesus who was to be sacrificed for our sins. In Genesis 22:2-4, it says:

> [God said] *"Take now your son, your only son Isaac, whom you love, and go to the region of Moriah; and offer him there*

as a burnt offering." So Abraham rose early in the morning, saddled his donkey, and took two of his young men with him and his son Isaac; and he split the wood for the burnt offering, and then began the trip to the place of which God had told him. On the third day Abraham looked up and saw the place in the distance.

This "place in the distance" was the victory of the Lord, His cross and resurrection, as well as the third day that Jesus spoke about in Luke 13:32. In John 8:56, Jesus said, "Your father Abraham rejoiced to see my day: and he saw it, and was glad" (KJV). This is the third day; the day of which the Lord was speaking. It's important to note that Solomon's temple represented, in part, God's permanent dwelling with men and that it was built in the same place on Mount Moriah where Abraham took Isaac as a sacrifice. This event foreshadowed the sacrifice that Christ would later make, which provided for *all* of God's children to become that permanent dwelling place (replacing the function of the temple).

Here are some more passages that relate to the *third day:*

*On the **third day** Esther put on her royal robes and stood in the inner court of the palace, in front of the king's hall. The king was sitting on his royal throne in the hall, facing the entrance* (Esther 5:1 NIV).

Here, Esther gained entrance before the King, saving the Jewish people from destruction *on the third day* of her fast. In Second Kings, when King Hezekiah faces death, he begs the Lord to heal him. Isaiah returns with the message that he will be healed and that he is to go up to the house of the Lord on *the third day* (see 2 Kings 20:1-11). Also, Joshua leads the people of Israel into the Promised Land *three days* after the Lord establishes him as Moses' replacement. After the Lord speaks to Joshua, he tells the officers,

*Go through the camp and tell the people, 'Get your supplies
ready. **Three days** from now you will cross the Jordan here to
go in and take possession of the land the Lord your God is giving you for your own* (Joshua 1:11 NIV).

Within these Scriptures are examples of standing before our King
in royal robes, receiving our healing, entering into the house of
God, and entering into the Promised Land.

These are only a few examples of *third day* types, which point
to actual events that are ripe and ready to manifest as the *seventh*
day and the *third* day approach. Jesus said, "Go ye, and tell that
fox, 'Behold, I cast out devils, and I do cures *today and tomorrow*,
and the *third day* I shall be perfected'" (Luke 13:32 KJV). In this
passage, *today* and *tomorrow* represent the last 2,000 years since
His death and resurrection. The third day is now upon us, and it
is the very day that He calls the Day of the Lord, in which the
greatest and most significant move of God in all of human history
will take place (see Matt. 13:30, Rev. 14:14-17). It's just around
the corner, literally within the blink of an eye.

Isaiah prophesied this long ago:

*Those who belong to God will live; their bodies will rise again!
Those who sleep in the earth will rise and sing for joy! For
God's light of life will fall like dew on His people in the place
of the dead* (Isaiah 26:19 NLT).

Hosea also spoke of the entrance into the coming age when he
wrote, "After two days He will revive us (quicken us, give us life);
on the third day He will raise us up that we may live before Him
(Hos. 6:2). Two days have passed since Jesus' resurrection. He has
quickened us with renewal, and He is now going to bring us
worldwide revival. Truly, on the third day we shall live before
Him. Hallelujah!

CHAPTER 9

The Day of the Lord

L et's set the record straight once and for all. God is a God of power, restoration, reconciliation, and love. The Church is not getting ready to shrink back and suffer curses and judgments. The Lord is not coming back for a weak and power-less Church, whimpering to be delivered from the antichrist evils. Rather, He is coming for a Bride that has overcome evil with good (see Rom. 12:21). The devil isn't going to go out quietly, but we are not going to be under his feet; he will be under ours (see Rom. 16:20). Be of great courage and persevere until the end, for you are more than a conqueror in Christ Jesus (see Rom. 8:37).

The Church is walking in much greater authority now than we ever were before. We hear reports from our beloved five-fold evangelists ministering over seas that miracles, signs, and won-ders are on the increase and conversions are multiplying daily, especially in third world countries. The latest worldwide daily conversion estimate I've heard was an average of 200,000 peo-ple per day are receiving the Lord! We wonder why we see the dead being raised, the sick healed, and thousands of salvations occurring in places like Africa, *while here in America* we seem to be at a stand still. Well, America's turn is right around the corner.

It occurs to me as I write that much of the Church in the third world has had to remain underground. That same issue is now being discussed at large in America. Could persecution of Christians begin to happen? I think not! Great changes have been affecting the Church, and it has been making everyone uneasy. The anointing has shifted into strategic regional gatherings intended to release impartation, preparing the Bride for the battles ahead and the flood of glory that will accompany them. Meanwhile, the Sunday-camp dwellers are being scattered and house churches are popping up all over the place.

It seems very evident that God is getting ready to bust a move in America. We are being prepared to host a revival such as the world has never seen. I believe that God has saved America as His trump card. He has saved the best wine for last, as He is accustomed to doing. I believe that the Lord is going to pour out a drink of the Holy Spirit through America that will cause the nations to come to the brightness of her rising! Many of the nations are already here in America. In Isaiah 56:7, the Lord declares through the prophet that His house shall be called a house of prayer for all peoples. Am I being presumptuous? Could the Lord be planning to use America as the flint that starts a global "one new man," burning for Jesus? I can't prove it, but I can declare that I believe it! I believe that there are more people per capita in America who love Jesus than anywhere else in the entire world. He would have spared Sodom for a handful!

All this talk about doom and gloom for America is nothing short of unbiblical. However, you can be sure that God is a just God and He is bringing judgment. He will judge sickness and disease, and healing will be the sentence! He will judge the spirit of poverty, and provision to advance His Kingdom will be the sentence! He will judge sin and lawlessness, and an unprecedented wave of kindness and grace will bring about mass repentance and salvation! He will judge religion and the religious spirit, and an outpouring of the Holy Spirit will destroy the structures and agendas of men, leaving the victorious church floating freely atop the flood waters of glory!

The nations have all flocked here over the years as if the stage was being set for a grand finale of revivals that will rival anything we have ever seen. I believe that the power and glory revealed in America will be part of what makes the Jews jealous, and then it shall be Jerusalem's turn to arise and shine (see Isaiah 60:1-2, Zech. 8:23). In these days, the "one new man" will be realized; Jew and Gentile will worship the Lord together, and the promised land will be overflowing with believers from many nations, Egyptians and Assyrians alike (see Isa. 19:23-25).

I'm now going to take you through an unusual scenario of the Day of the Lord, beginning with this scripture in Luke:

> For like the lightning, that flashes and lights up the sky from one end to the other, so will the Son of Man be in His [own] day (Luke 17:24).

The "Day of the Lord" will come suddenly, without warning, but there will be an era which precedes this day, where the Lord will be revealed through His Church. The glory of the Lord will first be revealed through His Bride (see Eph. 3:9-11), and then He will come with all of the saints that went on before us. He will come to resurrect the dead, and we who remain on the earth at that time will be changed into our glorified bodies. We shall be caught up in the *clouds* to meet with the Lord in the air (see 1 Thess. 4:17), which I believe indicates that He will come with the saints that went on before us (see Rev. 19:14, 1 Thess. 3:13, Jude 14). These saints are the great *cloud* of witnesses (see Heb. 12:1). First Thessalonians 4:17 says, "Then we which are alive and remain shall be caught up together with them in the clouds, to meet the Lord in the air: and so shall we ever be with the Lord" (KJV).

To meet the Lord in the air, as it says in this Scripture, indicates an action rather than a place. It doesn't mean that we will meet Him in the literal air above; rather, it indicates that we will meet Him in the process of a specific action. The word *air* in this Scripture is spelled aer in the Greek, and is a verb, rather than a noun, which means "to breathe unconsciously, i.e. respire, [or] to blow as naturally *circumambient*."[1] The Webster's definition of *circumambient* is to "surround in a circle, surrounding or encompassing."[2] Now, *aer* is also defined as the atmosphere, but in this case, not the literal air above. Rather, this atmosphere is a surrounding influence or environment. Remember, the key part of the definition of *aer*, that it is circumambient, which means to surround in a circle and to be encompassing.

To clarify this, I will quote from a sermon delivered by Brian Simmons, senior pastor of Gateway Christian Fellowship in West Haven, Connecticut, who was speaking at a worship conference that Judith and I hosted at the Sturbridge Worship Center in Sturbridge, Massachusetts.

I am beginning to wonder if intercession is somehow a mingling of the prophetic, the priestly, and the kingly ministries, over-lapping as those three kingdom ministries merge.

True intercessors are prophetic. They see what God's hand is about to do, like the sons of Issachar. They knew the times. They knew what Israel was about to do. They were few in number, but every one of them had influence. They were chiefs, it says, they were captains, every one of them.

Intercessors have a perception of what's coming, so they are in that regard prophetic, but they are also priests. The High Priest came wearing the breastplate with twelve stones over his heart. He brought them constantly before God. Intercessors never come only for themselves. Those who have been called and gripped by a spirit of supplication are those who come carrying the people of God on their heart. Like Paul, they labor in travail till God be formed in the womb of the hearts of men. There is a true loving of the people of God that is released. An intercessor must be a priest. He or she must have a priestly care for the flock and the people of God. So they are prophetic and have a measure of priestly and prophetic activity.

But there is also that kingly, regal authority that declares and pulls down the kingdom of God into the earth. An intercessor brings the future into the present.

An intercessor escorts the will of God to the earth. They are like painters, who paint a bulls-eye on the promise of God and say, "Strike it now Lord, with your power. Strike it now. Bring your power down now Lord!"

So you see, an intercessor is somehow a conglomeration; kind of a no-bake cookie of all those ingredients. The heart of the intercessor becomes the *womb* where God's purpose labors to come forth. He or she is a focused warrior who conspires together with God. To conspire means to *breathe* [aer] together. Again, to conspire means to *breathe* [aer] together. The intercessor breathes with God. At the right hand of God, leaning on His breast, hearing His heartbeat, we begin to breathe out the very words and prophetic promises of the Lord.

Acts 9:1 says, "Meanwhile Saul, still drawing his breath hard from threatening and murderous desire against the disciples of the Lord, went to the high priest." So you see, Saul at this time is conspiring with Satan. He draws his breath or breathes in Satan's hateful plots, and then breathes out the evil threats and murderous desires against the disciples of the Lord. But the intercessor *breathes* out the words and purposes of God.

There's a conspiring and breathing together with God and man. There's a partnership in prayer that God wants to bring His end-time's church into, where we put an end to our silly *religious* prayers and we begin to pray *Holy Ghost* prayers! We begin to pray in fellowship and in harmony with the breath of God, the wind of God. There's a wind blowing and I say, blow it through my prayers, Lord! Breathe it in me, God!

So, we breathe together with God. We are in heart-to-heart communion with Him. Of course, our worship and intercession is a pale version of the kind of communion we will have with Him when He comes. When He returns we will meet with the Lord in the aer. He will come with the host of Heaven and surround the earth with a circumambient force of power. He's coming for a Bride with whom He will *consummate*. When we consummate with Him, He shall *consume* us. The word consume means to be totally burned up and reduced to nothing.[3] Thus, our carnal nature will be consumed, and we will experience the literal induction of the Lord's total nature. Now grab a hold of this: the word *induction* means:

The act or process of reasoning from a part to a whole, from the individual to the universal. Also the process by which an electrical conductor becomes electrified when near a charged body [proximity anointing transfer], by which a magnetizable body [Body of Christ], becomes magnetized when in a magnetic field, or in the magnetic flux, set up by a magneto-motive force [Holy Spirit].[4]

To clarify the application of this definition, I inserted the parallel spiritual meaning in brackets. The magneto-motive force is the Holy Spirit, the breath of God, the light of life. His electric life completely regenerates His people into the perfect image of Christ, our husband-to-be. Our natural flesh and our carnal nature shall evaporate, as it were, and be consumed in the fire of God, that all-consuming fire.

The sun causes the water on the earth to become a vapor. The water yields to the sun's power, rising to form a cloud, which then produces rain. Since all things in the natural are a shadow and a type of the things in the spirit, what does this natural process represent in the real and spiritual realm? Just as the sun interacts with water, so also the fire of God consumes our carnal nature, causing us to become completely yielded to His Spirit, thus changing us into the pure likeness of Christ. The fullness of the Bride of Christ becomes like a great mass or cloud. The Hebrew word for *cloud* in 1 Kings 18:44 is *awb*, which means "a density, a thick cloud, or thicket-like clay."[5] I believe that this thicket of clay is the Bride of Christ, through whom the rain of the Spirit will pour forth abundantly.

In this passage of First Kings, Elijah sent his servant to look for rain *seven* times. On the seventh time, which I believe represents the *seventh* day of fallen man, the servant reported, "Behold, there ariseth a little cloud out of the sea, *like* a man's hand" (1 Kings 18:44 KJV). The sea here represents the world and this cloud is *like* a man's hand. Consider the hand of a man having five phalanges. This cloud that is *like* a man's hand is a metaphorical representation of the five spiritual offices of the Church; a picture of the restored five-fold Church. This restored Church will usher in the *rains of the Spirit*. For this little cloud that arises out of the sea prophesies of the latter rain of the Spirit that will pour forth through the reformed Church of Christ in the Day of the Lord. This *awb*, cloud, or thicket-like clay is the Bride of Christ. So, shall we be caught up in the clouds together? We shall be like a great cloud! But what about the great cloud of witnesses, the clouds that come with the Lord when He returns? He comes with the clouds of Heaven, it says in Scripture. I believe that the former (the cloud of the previous Saints) and the latter (the cloud of the "Day of the Lord" Saints) shall rain together. Now that's a new twist on an old theme.

In Jude 12 it says that the wicked are "clouds without rain" or water. But we, the righteous, are clouds with rain, the rain of the Spirit. I believe that the latter rain shall come in great and enormous cloudbursts and soak the entire world with the knowledge of the glory of the Lord. The Bride of Christ shall become the oracle of the Lord. The latter rain of the Spirit and the Bridal shower revivals in these last days shall be the greatest move of God ever recorded in human history. The Lord has put a diamond ring on the finger of His Bride, and we are going to flaunt that ring all over the world. Upon the black backdrop of a dark and dying world shall arise a shining Bride declaring Christ with signs and wonders following, and the testimony of our unity will be our diadem!

So, the former and the latter shall rain together, and when the dead are raised, the former and the latter saints shall *reign* together with the Lord. We shall *rain* together, and we shall *reign* together with the Lord. We shall for all of eternity conspire with the Lord for His purposes. He is the King of kings, and we shall be prophets, priests, and kings unto Him. Imagine co-laboring with God forever as His Bride, endowed with power.

The stage has been set; the foundation has been laid. The Lord will manifest through His people with resurrection life all over the world. The Day of the Lord is at hand. We have entered into what Jesus called the third day. Jesus said in Luke 13:32, "Go ye, and tell that fox, behold, I cast out devils, and do cures today and tomorrow, and the *third day* I shall be perfected" (KJV). The surface theology here is that Jesus rose from the dead on the *third* day. That's very important; He was glorified on that day. But this passage reveals even more than the day of *His* resurrection; it also reveals the day of *our* resurrection. Remember the Scripture where Peter says that a day is as a thousand years with the Lord, and a thousand years is as one day (see 2 Pet. 3:8). This clearly shows us that when Jesus says "today and tomorrow" in Luke 13, He's speaking of the next two thousand years, the Church age. So you see, He continued to do miracles and cast out devils through us, His Bride, for the last two thousand years. "And the *third day* I shall be perfected," He says. This is a millennial statement the Lord is making here. Remember Hosea 6:2, which says, "After two days He will revive us (quicken us, give us life); on the *third day* He will *raise* us up that we may live before Him."

It is interesting that the number *three* represents fullness, which concerning us, the Bride, means "the requisite or complete amount, and fully developed or mature; having attained complete status."[6] It also represents the fullness of the Godhead and the fullness of time, the fullness of the restoration of all things spoken by the mouth of God's holy prophets. Isn't it wonderfully interesting how it coincides and harmonizes with the meaning of the number seven (perfection), which we discussed earlier? It's also interesting that the word perfected is used in Luke 13:32 in the first place, since the numbers *three* and *seven* have similar and harmonious meanings. The number *seven* represents perfection, and Jesus is talking about being perfected on the *third* day. It's also interesting that the word *perfected* was translated from the Greek word *teleloo*, which means "to consummate."[7] With whom is He going to consummate? To whom is He getting married? We just studied what the word *consummate* means: to be consumed by the fire of God, our carnal nature being reduced to nothing so that we can be *perfected* in the Spirit. You see, we also come into *our* perfection in Him. This is a two-way deal. It's a marriage!

It is beyond exciting to see how this all comes together. We will meet Him in the *aer* as Heaven surrounds the earth with a circumambient force of power; we then will attain *fullness* and each be *perfected* on the *third* day; we will consummate and experience the *induction* of Heaven's reality as He comes with the clouds (saints) of Heaven; the former and the latter saints shall rain/reign together; and this all occurs on the *third* and the *seventh* day!

The most exciting thing is that He reveals this to us in the Scriptures, but you have to search it out. He's hiding treasures through-out the word for us to find, much like a father hides special gifts around the house for his children to find and delight in. Proverbs 25:2 explains, "It is the glory of God to conceal a thing, but the glory of kings is to search out a thing."

Of course, Jesus Christ is already perfect, but He is not complete without His Bride. When He says, "I shall be perfected," He refers to our mutual wedding day and the *consummation* of our spiritual wedlock with one another. He then becomes complete, just as we become complete. Oh yes, on the *third day* He rose from the dead after His body lay in the tomb. While He was there, He witnessed to the dead in Hades, and they rose from the dead right after Him, and went out into the streets of the Holy City and witnessed to many (see Matt. 27:51-53). At the appointed time, on the *third day*, the second coming of Christ will arrive and the dead will again be raised. Even now, there are many reports of the dead being raised throughout the world, just like Lazarus.[8] However, on the day of the Lord's glorious return, *all* those who sleep in Christ, whose tombs are filled with ashes, will burst forth with spiritual life and meet with the Lord in the air (aer).

Of course, history will repeat itself at the end of the age. Yes, the Lord is omnipresent, and He shall be seen through us as we mirror His image in the earth before He returns. But He shall also be seen personally by all of creation when He returns, just as literally as the Bible explains it. Perhaps we will meet Him in the literal air above as well. However, let us be positively sure of this: He's not coming on the cumulus clouds of the earth that are filled with acid rain. He's coming with the clouds of Heaven! You can be sure that when He returns with all the saints who went on before us (the great cloud of witnesses), to join with His perfected latter rain Bride, that the earth will have a circumambient force of Heaven's power surrounding it.

Earlier I alluded to the idea that all of the words spoken through the mouths of God's prophets will come into their fulfillment when the Lord returns. I'll cover that with Scripture in a moment. But let me say this: just as all things had to be in order and fully prepared for the *rains* that would come for forty days and forty nights to flood the earth in Noah's day, so also must all things be ready and prepared for the return of Jesus and the *rains of the Spirit* that will flood the earth. Acts 3:21 speaks of Jesus, saying, "Whom the heaven must receive until *the times* of restitution of all things, which God hath spoken by the mouth of all His holy prophets since the world began" (KJV). So, you see, His Church will be fully restored when He returns. The issue of "all things" is explained in the text where it says that He is coming in "the times" of restitution. There is an overlapping of what will be restored before He returns and what will be restored during and after His return. This is no small thing. All things prophesied by the Lord's prophets in Scripture must come to pass *as* the Lord returns for His people. We are in those times right now.

There were six days of creation, and on the seventh day the Lord rested. I believe that we have reached the end of the sixth millennial day of fallen man and that we have already passed through the crux and entered into the seventh day and the times of restitution. In this seventh day, all of the Church shall enter into the Lord's perfect rest. I believe that the Tabernacle of David restored will be used by the Holy Spirit to produce unity in the Body of Christ worldwide and bring completion to the "one new man" burning for Jesus. In unity, we will keep the fire burning, producing a cataclysmic spiritual explosion of God's power demonstrated by the Church. We shall usher in the second coming of our Lord, the resurrection of the dead, the induction of the fullness of the Lord's prayer ("Thy Kingdom come, Thy will be done, in earth as it is in Heaven"), and the dawning of the millennial reign with Christ. This will be the fullness of the seventh and third day, when all things will be reconciled back to the Lord. All of the earth will be filled with the knowledge of the glory of the Lord, just as it is now in Heaven! Let the Bride make herself ready!

CHAPTER 10

Revelation of the Bride and the Groom

J ust as surely as we are seated with Christ in heavenly places, so also, Christ fills our earthen vessels. This is why (as bond servants) we have His authority to do the "greater works" that He told us about (see John 14:12). We are filled with His glory! How big is your mustard seed? (See Matthew 17:20.) The prayer of Jesus is enough to make you take leaps of faith. His word alone is the seed that bears much fruit. His word alone imputes and ascribes to us the gift of faith that is from God and performs the will of God. Jesus prayed:

> *Neither for these alone do I pray [it is not for their sake only that I make this request], but also for all those who will ever come to believe in (trust in, cling to, rely on) Me through their word and teaching, That they all may be one, [just] as You, Father, are in Me and I in You, that they also may be one in Us, so that the world may believe and be convinced that You have sent Me. I have given to them the glory and honor which You have given Me, that they may be one [even] as We are one: I in them and You in Me, in order that they may become one and perfectly united, that the world may*

know and [definitely] recognize that You sent Me and that
You have loved them [even] as You have loved Me (John
17:20-23).

My goodness, according to these words, there is nothing that
can't be accomplished through Christ Jesus who lives and reigns
in us! Take hold of the revelation of Jesus inhabiting His worshiping Bride, and let the glories of life in the Spirit of God keep you
on the path of victory. Let us go from one degree of glory to
another! Press in. Abide in the vine and let His River overflow the
banks!

If you haven't guessed it already, you probably will at this
point. Judith is a dreamer, a seer, and a visionary. I want to share
another of her dreams. If I was to tell you all of her dreams and
visions, I would have to dedicate an entire book just to those
experiences. This dream-vision ties the subjects of this book
together very neatly. Everything that we have been talking about
becomes more than just a good teaching; it takes on a life of its
own as this revelation unfolds. Jesus reveals His heart for us and
His intentions to inhabit Judah in a remarkable way. Truly, we are
coming very close to His return. The Lord is becoming more tan-
gibly present in our worship experiences, and He will only
increase this drama as we approach the grand finale.

In Judith's revelatory dream-vision experience, it was com-
monly known that there was a prophet and two of his helpers visiting church bodies in our region of New England. However, in
Judy's mind, she had the understanding and revelation that these
guys were really Jesus and two angels visiting the churches while
remaining *anonymous*. There are multiple examples of the Lord visiting chosen individuals throughout Scripture. Just to name a few, He
came as Melchizedek the pre-incarnate Christ (see Gen. 14:18-20),

as the *Angel of the Lord* to Gideon (see Judg. 6:11), as the risen Christ to the disciples on the road to Emmaus (see Luke 24:13-32), and as the high and exalted King who visited John on the island of his exile. (See the Book of Revelation.) Will the Lord bodily visit His Church unaware? We know of the Scripture that speaks of entertaining angels unaware (see Heb. 13:2). Is Jesus still the Angel of the Lord? Of course He is. The Lord will indeed visit His people in bodily form as He has in the past.[1] He will visit many people, revealing Himself to some and remaining anonymous to others. There have already been many testimonies to this.[2] My friends Danny Steyne and Irving King are two such people that have had this privilege. The Lord visited with His people in bodily form throughout biblical history and has also visited His people throughout the Church age. So don't be surprised when He turns up the volume and visits us more frequently in the days ahead. The prophets, including Danny Steyne, have declared that He will do this more and more as the time draws near to His second coming in glory.

The Lord has promised my wife Judah that He will visit her soon. He's already visited her once, and He's promised to visit her again. When He came to her the first time, He came sobbing, saying, "The tender grapes on the vine are being trampled upon and bruised by My own people. I paid the price for all to put on the garments of salvation by faith. I long for My people to approach Me without cringing fear. Tell My people I love them; just tell them I love them."

In part of Judith's dream, Wayne Anderson was ministering at our church. He gave Judith that specific look and twinkle of the eye that is distinguishing to him. They simply agreed in the Spirit that Jesus was coming to the church personally. Thus Jesus came; and when He did, He arrived *unannounced* and began to prophesy to certain people. As He spoke and performed miracles, they would fall under His power. Then He suddenly clapped His hands, and Judith was instantly taken into a realm of timelessness. She was taken by the Lord out of her ordinary dream state and was transported into a spiritual realm much like that of a trance. In this state of timelessness, she saw that, as Jesus clapped His hands together and then opened them, a great sphere appeared between His hands. It was the heavenly sphere. Within this sphere was all of the Lord's creation, all of the constellations, and all of the heavenly realms. Everything that He had ever created, she witnessed all at once. All of creation unfolded before her eyes as on a spherical video screen.

After gazing upon this for a time, she was then taken out of that trance-like state and was placed back into her ordinary dream state. When this happened, she noticed that the Lord was preparing to leave the church unannounced. She approached Him, and as she did, He asked her, "May I come to your next meeting and worship the Father with you?" (Do you not know that the Lord is always knocking on the door? He's always asking permission for entrance.) Elated as she was, she replied yes, and asked Him, "Do you play a trumpet?" The Lord answered, "Yes, Yes I do." She secretly knew that this was the Lord, yet she remained pensive and wondering. The implication here is that the Lord Himself wanted to lead us into worshiping our heavenly Father and to inhabit the praises of His people. He will indeed be doing this all over the world, interacting with us in an immensely intimate and even romantic way.

This coming and going of the Lord is like an ebb and a flow; coming in unannounced and going out unannounced. It's like an inhaling and an exhaling of the Spirit, where we breathe (aer) in the encompassing presence of the Lord, then breath (aer) out the prophetic promises of the Father to flood the earth with His glory and revival fire. We studied earlier concerning this matter of breathing in the Spirit, conspiring with God, and meeting with the Lord in the air (aer). We will breathe in the desires of the Father's heart and breathe out the prophetic promises and intentions of the Father concerning them. It's all like a holy rhythm. He's bringing His Church into a holy rhythm of spiritual intimacy. In our quiet chambers, we will enjoy a most beautiful spiritual intimacy. While in the public arena, He will sing with us, He will dance with us, and He will spin us about. He will send the wind of His Spirit to blow through our hair, which represents our faithfulness to Him, which will be like the New Jerusalem's flag waving freely in the face of the enemy.

When Judith woke up from this dream, she went straight to the Lord to spend a great deal of time in prayer. He then led her to many Scriptures that confirmed what this vision meant. In Ephesians it says:

Also to enlighten all men and make plain to them what is the plan [regarding the Gentiles and providing for the salvation of all men] of the mystery kept hidden through the ages and concealed until now in [the mind of] God who created all things by Christ Jesus. [The purpose is] that through the church the complicated, many-sided wisdom of God in all its infinite variety and innumerable aspects might now be made known to the angelic rulers and authorities (principalities and powers) in the heavenly sphere. This is in accordance with the terms of the eternal and timeless purpose which He has realized and carried into effect in [the person of] Christ Jesus our Lord (Ephesians 3:9-11).

It says that "this is in accordance with the terms of the eternal and *timeless* purpose...." Judith was taken into a place of *timelessness* where she witnessed this *heavenly sphere*. Our worship and intercession cuts through the barriers of time and space and has a direct impact in the heavenly realms.

This is one of the most intense confirmations of a dream or vision that I've ever seen or heard. Jesus will in fact declare, *through the Church*, His scope of total sovereignty over all things to the principalities and powers. Literally, all of who He is and all of who *we are in Him* shall be revealed through the Bride to the principalities and powers in the *heavenly sphere* that Judith saw in her vision. This heavenly sphere of all He created includes the principalities and powers. As Paul wrote:

> For it was in Him that all things were created, in heaven and on earth, things seen and things unseen, whether thrones, dominions, rulers, or authorities; all things were created and exist through Him [by His service, intervention] and in and for Him. And He Himself existed before all things, and in Him all things consist (cohere, and are held together) (Colossians 1:16–17).

This passage provides yet another confirmation of the vision of Jesus holding in His very hands all that He has ever created, exercising His sovereign control and authority over all of it. All things were created by Him and for Him, and they exist and are held together by the power of His word. If He were to withhold His word for one moment, everything would cease to exist. He is God, and He has all things prepared for reconciliation and restoration. The passage continues,

> And God purposed that through [by the service, the intervention of) Him [the Son] all things should be completely

*reconciled back to Himself, whether on earth or in heaven, as through Him, [the Father] made peace by means of **the blood of His cross** (Colossians 1:20).*

All things will be reconciled back to the Lord. All who belong to Him, all who are called to inherit eternal life, and all of creation itself will be reconciled back to the Lord Jesus Christ, who brought them all into existence. The Lord brought Judith to one other Scripture:

Then the [mighty] angel whom I had seen stationed on sea and land raised his right hand to heaven (the sky), And swore in the name of (by) Him Who lives forever and ever, Who created the heavens (sky) and all they contain, and the earth and all that it contains, and the sea and all that it contains. [He swore] that no more time should intervene and there should be no more waiting or delay, But that when the days come when the trumpet call of the seventh angel is about to be sounded, then God's mystery (His secret design, His hidden purpose), as He had announced the glad tidings to his servants the prophets, should be fulfilled (accomplished, completed) (Revelation 10:5-7).

The time for the fulfillment of the words of His prophets is here. The time for *all things* to be reconciled back to Him has arrived! The times of the "restitution of all things" are upon us. God's mystery and hidden purposes are ready to take the enemy off guard and propel His Church into battle with fresh manna. The battlefield of worship is lit up with fireworks and the trumpet has sounded loud and clear!

The Lord inhabits the praises of His people, leading us into the worship of the Father. Prophetic worship, filled with intercession, will bring forth the songs of His heart to the Father, songs for the lost, the needy, the sick, the broken, and the oppressed. This activity will burn like wildfire, and through it all, God's mystery (His secret design and hidden purpose) shall be fulfilled, accomplished, and completed. Praise the Lord! Hebrews says, "For He (Jesus) says, I will declare Your [the Father's] name to My brethren; in the midst of the [worshiping] congregation *I* will sing hymns of praise to *You*" (Heb. 2:12). Jesus is going to give us the songs that will bless the Father's heart; both spontaneous and composed prophetic songs. We, as a multitude, will permeate the *atmosphere* with the mediation of Jesus to the Father.

In Psalms it says, "My heart is inditing a good matter: I speak of the things *which I have made* touching the king: my tongue is the pen of a ready writer" (Ps. 45:1 KJV). Our Father declares that His heart overflows with a good matter, and that He speaks concerning the King. The term *good matter* is from the root Hebrew word *dabar* and literally means "word."[3] The good *Word* is King Jesus Himself. Jesus *is* the Word. Our Father recites His composition (poem) to the King, the Word of life. What beauty it is to see the Father giving glory to the Son and the Son giving glory to the Father. This is the way it has always been from the beginning and ever shall be for eternity. In Proverbs 8:30-31, Jesus rejoices before the Father and is the absolute delight of the Father. All the while, the delight of Jesus is with the sons of men. He rejoiced in His "inhabited world," as the New King James Version says. He was spinning and dancing and *halaling* over us as He created His masterpiece universe! The ecstatic God twirled and danced and propelled life from His very being while shouting exaltations with thundering symphonies too great to mention.

There was a finished and satisfied end to God's plan from the very beginning, and it was God the Son, slain from the foundation of the world. The very pinnacle of His joy was realized in His cross. Truly, for the joy set before Him, he suffered (see Heb. 12:2).

The psalmist wrote:

Your throne, O God, is forever and ever; a scepter of right-eousness is the scepter of Your kingdom. You love righteous-ness and hate wickedness; therefore God, Your God, has anointed You with the oil of gladness more than Your compan-ions (Psalm 45:6-7 NKJV).

Our God the Father has anointed our God the Son with the oil of gladness, and this is where we draw our strength from. The joy of the Lord will be our strength and our testimony in times of tribulation. The very exhibition of this joy publicly will have the anointing to draw in the harvest.

Psalm 45 goes on to prophesy of our inheritance:

Listen, O daughter [**bride**], *consider and incline your ear; forget your own people also, and your father's house; [forsake all and follow Him] so the King will greatly desire your beauty; because He is your Lord, worship Him. And the daughter of Tyre* [**Bride of the Rock, God**] *will come with a gift; the rich among the people will seek your favor. The royal daughter* [**Bride**] *is all glorious within the palace; her clothing is woven with gold. She shall be brought to the King* [**Jesus**] *in robes of many colors; the virgins* [**last great har-vest**], *her companions who follow her, shall be brought to You. With gladness and rejoicing they shall be brought; they shall enter the King's palace. Instead of Your fathers shall be Your sons, whom You shall make princes* [**co-rulers**] *in all the earth. I* [**the Father**] *will make Your name to be remem-bered in all generations; therefore the people shall praise You forever and ever* (Psalm 45:10-17 NKJV).

I added the words in brackets to bring clarity to what this Scripture is telling us. This is our inheritance. We will enter into glory, our newly saved companions following after us. All those who cry out at the sound of last trumpet will rejoice with intense fervor. Can you imagine looking over the balcony of hell and being whisked away into glory? Wow! What an entrance! Jesus gets the last laugh on earth, and we will all laugh for eternity thereafter!

Let there be no more waiting, Lord! Let there be no more delay. Come quickly, Lord! You have knocked on the door of Your Church and on the door of our hearts. Like the beloved, our hands drip with myrrh (see Song of Sol. 5:5). We open the door unto You, Lord God. Your beloved desires to ride with You now, in Your day of power. We will offer ourselves willingly Lord in the day of Your power. Like the beloved, we say,

> Come, my beloved! Let us go forth into the field, let us lodge in the villages. Let us go out early to the vineyards and see whether the vines have budded, whether the grape blossoms have opened, and whether the pomegranates are in bloom. There I will give you my love (Song of Solomon 7:11-12).

Let us ravish Your heart, Lord God, in this hour! Let Your sister, Your promised Bride, ravish Your heart (see Song of Sol. 4:9). Amen and Amen!

Summary Prayer

Bride of Christ, arise and shine, for your light has come! Today is the day of salvation. Today is the day to praise the Lord. Darkness and great darkness has covered the earth, but like a diamond on a black backdrop, we shine with the glory of the Lord. Worship the King, and reveal His glory to the nations. Let the roar of the Lord be heard from Zion! The greatest awakening of all time is upon us, and we are to be prepared to ride the wave. We are to be ready with the God of power who lives inside of us. We are to be ready, in the great day of His manifested power, to give of ourselves willingly. Let the worshipers be released from the bonds that keep them from adorning the gates of Heaven with praise.

The Tabernacle of David is being restored in our very midst as we speak. The Lord and His harvest await us all at the Gate Beautiful. A great host of prophets, priests, and kings shall be released into the Gate Beautiful battlefields of worship. Armies of Gideon arise and take your post. Let freedom reign in your hearts. Let the worshipers from every denomination be quickened in their Spirit man, and let them lay down their lives prostrate before the Lord of hosts. Let us set ourselves ablaze, and let the world come and see us burn. Tear down the altars of religion in our hearts so that we may burn with the fires of true worship. Release the sounds of Heaven and rejoice in the magnificent salvation of our God!

Rebuild and reform Your Church, Lord Jesus. Bring genuine unity of mind and Spirit to your Body. Manifest the answer of Your prayer in John 17, that the entire world would see our unity. Let the remainder of Israel become jealous. May the hearts of Israel be turned to Jesus, and let the one new man be realized in this hour! Release Your mercy, Lord, and let the multitudes tremble in the wake of Your glory! For Your mercy is great, and only those that you have called can stand in the light of it. Let Your mercy triumph over judgment in this hour, Lord, so that a great harvest will be won for Your name's sake.

Fill worship with a call to the nations, that they will bow according to Your word. Let every knee bow and every tongue confess that Jesus is Lord. We see a little cloud that is like a man's hand, and we hear the sound of the abundance of rain. Let the former and the latter rain soak the earth with Your glorious presence, and let Your people reign together with You in harmony and great power. Restore us to the garden of purity, and let us share in the tree of life. We long to be ready in and out of season with healing hands, Lord. Plant us by Your River of delights, and let our lives yield eternal fruit. Let resurrection life be released over the nations! Breathe on us, oh God, with Your breath of life afresh, and fan the smoking flax. Revive Your Church, and restore us to the oneness that we had in the upper room. Give us the boldness of Acts 4:29-30. Release Your word through us, and let miracles, signs, and wonders follow us, so that Your word will be established and confirmed.

Summary Prayer

And finally Lord, inhabit Judah. Come and establish a mercy seat throughout the earth. Give us the songs that will set the world ablaze for You, and bless us with Your tangible presence. Manifest Yourself over us according to Your word. Release the sounds from Heaven that will prophetically declare Your love, Your everlasting grace, and Your mercy which endures forever and ever! Amen and Amen.

Study Guide

Because this book is designed as a study guide, I have only included questions in this study that can place you *personally* in the events of the book. It was my intention to make this study conducive to group study, although doing it alone will also be beneficial. I have included answers to the questions, which are listed on the page directly following the questions. Be disciplined and *do not* turn the page to peak at them before you give your answer. These answers cover a general scope of information as they pertain to groups of gifting or kingdom scenarios. For instance, an answer may be directed to intercessors in general, but only *you* can personalize the answer. Write your answers down in the space between the questions, and then compare them to the general answers on the next page.

Chapter 1 Questions

1. Are you a gate? Why or why not?

2. Do you feel led to take part in the last great harvest? If yes, how do you see yourself taking action?

3. What has God put on your heart to be in the times that are just ahead?

Chapter 1 Answers

1. Every single person that belongs to Jesus is a gate. Your personalized answer depends upon your own walk with God. We are all called to *be* royal priests before the Lord. If you answered, "No I am not a gate," you may feel that you are not a gate because you are not a worship leader or an intercessor or some other kind of minister that has a platform. *This is not biblical.* Are you a Christian mother? Then *you are a gate* to your children. The degree to which you commit your mothering to Christ dictates how effective a gate you are to your children. Do you worship Jesus? If you do, *then you are a gate.* Everyone that loves the Lord is a gate. Now you can determine what kind of a gatekeeper you will be.

2. Every Christian is called to take part. We know that many are called, but few are chosen (see Matt. 20:15-16). The chosen part of the equation is really up to us. We can *choose* to participate or we can *choose* to sit on the sideline. It's our decision to make. God longs to use each one of us.

3. Notice that I didn't ask what you felt led to *do.* If you feel a call on your heart to *be* a gift to the Body of Christ, then the formula is not doing; it is being. Everything that the Lord has given us individually is to help us *become a gift* to others. The idea of *doing* describes works fueled by a spirit of duty. You have probably heard the new age mantra, "we are not human beings, we are human's being." Well, they almost have it; they just need to add Jesus to the picture. *Jesus*, who dwells within, *is* the gift, and *we* are the vessel that the gift of His life will flow through. We are certainly being and not doing. Relationship with Jesus is a state of being. He is the doer.

Chapter 2 Questions

1. Describe in your own words what the restoration of the Tabernacle of David means to you?

2. The Lord's Prayer shows us that we take ground for the Kingdom with worship. What ground can you take for God with a surrendered heart in worship?

3. Worship leaders, as defined by their prophetic musical gifting, are to be separated unto the Lord. If you are not a musician, how do you see yourself as a worshiper, and what kind of effect do you envision having for the harvest as a worshiper?

4. Are you a watchman?

   If so, what's your target? What specific bull's eye are you aiming at with your intercession?

5. The veils of religion must be removed. This will be a hard question, but a necessary one for all; no one is exempt. What veil of your flesh serves as a hindrance to pure and spiritual worship in your life? In other words, what form of religion do you need to burn at the stake?

Chapter 2 Answers

1. Restoring the Tabernacle of David means restoring worship that prophetically mirrors the purposes of God and declares them 24/7. This will look different in different cultures and even in different individual lives. Your answer is a key to understanding how you personally might function as a prophet, priest, and king in this great work.

2. There are two types of ground that we can take: personal ground and community ground. In either case, the soil of the human heart is the ground that must be conquered. God's arm is not short that it cannot reach down and save. There will be corporate efforts to reach regions, and there will be individual efforts to reach families (for instance). How you will be used depends upon your willingness to submit to the Lord. Your answer will reveal your heart concerning this subject. There is no right or wrong answer.

3. The single most powerful worship time that I have ever experienced happened when the corporate anointing grew so strong that I, as the worship leader, had to *follow* the lead of the masses of worshipers, whose voices of perfect unity were reaching a crescendo of power. It was similar to what is described in Second Chronicles:

> *Indeed it came to pass, when the trumpeters and singers were as one, to make one sound to be heard in praising and thanking the Lord, and when they lifted up their voice with the trumpets and cymbals and instruments of music, and praised the Lord, saying: "For He is good, for His mercy endures forever," that the house, of the Lord, was filled with a cloud* (2 Chronicles 5:13 NKJV).

If you envision yourself as an observer, then that is what you will be; for as a man thinks in his heart, so is he (see Prov. 23:7). All of us, becoming one in unity of heart, mind, and purpose, will forge the key of David. This key unlocks the worshiping gates and will create a radical change in the atmosphere to win our cities!

4. Not all are called to be this kind of intercessor. This kind of ministry creates a vacuum within the person that must be filled. They are consumed with the task of interceding in specific ways according to what's in God's heart. These types of intercessors are like Anna. This woman was a widow of about eighty-four years who did not depart from the temple, but served God, fasting and praying night and day her whole life, longing for the redemption of Jerusalem (see Luke 2:36-37). If you are called to this kind of ministry, you will know it.

5. Tough question? How does one answer this? If you have made it all the way through this book, then you probably don't serve religion the way we usually think of it. But we all tend to get wrapped up in some form or pattern here and there. The best that we can do is to remain continually open to how God decides to move at any given moment, and then we must yield to it.

Music, for instance, is a vehicle, and not an end in itself, to worship. If I play the same song every day for a month, it would not become a religious pattern *providing* that I let God take it over. It will be different every time I play it, because the worship of the Lord is a two-way street. God Himself inhabits Judah (the worship of His people). When God breathes (*aer*) upon the worship, we enter into communion with His heart and flow prophetically with Him. When this happens, the worship band will begin to move as one spontaneous prophetic voice. This will happen not only with singing, but also with instruments; a spontaneous combustion of various compositions, which consist of multiple movements in contrasting forms and keys, begins to merge. This of course, is issued forth from the Lord; it is truly a heavenly sonata. A *contrasting* effect provides diversity of adjacent parts in color, emotion, and tone.

Before you know it, the whole gathering of people will begin to flow corporately in that same vein, and the music will become dim in comparison to the unity of hearts that are manifesting love with one great sound. This is where the *sound of Heaven* will be heard. It's not going to be manifested as some supernatural sound coming out of our instruments. The *instrument* of the human hearts gathered together will beat in unity with each other and with the King and produce this sound. This will be the very sound that will usher in a revival such as has never been seen before. The revival of the upper room will be paled by the revivals that are coming. What can hold this back? Clinging to our patterns and form and never allowing the Lord to infiltrate our worship. Music is *only* the launching pad. If a rocket ship never gets off the launching pad, it will fry the platform, burn out, and fall to the ground; it will never rocket to the heavens. When we allow ourselves to be heart-ready to flow with God, where ever He decides to take us, *religion* will no longer hinder us, and we will take off with the Lord to the Heavens.

Chapter 3 Questions

1. Are you a nomad/floater?

   If yes, chronicle your experiences that brought you to this decision.

2. Have you been persecuted for your gifting? Describe this.

Chapter 3 Answers

1. Many people have been frustrated with the political agenda of the Church. If you answered yes to this question, then in one way or another, church structure has probably been hindering your worship experience. You are not to be grieved over your efforts to seek out green pasture. It is a rare thing to find a church these days that enters into the kind of spiritual worship that you desire to plunge into. Of course, there are some that *do* exist, and they are worthy of support. There have been many church-splits in the name of freedom. Jesus, the peacemaker, showed up at Toronto, and like a genuine peacemaker, He uprooted and exposed the lies of the enemy and started a feud. It is not a peacemaker's job to cause evil and good to agree with one another. It is the peacemaker's job to expose lies by exampling the truth.

2. If you are a nomad/floater, it is possible that you were kicked out of your church for exercising your spiritual freedom in Christ through your spiritual gifts. Or perhaps worship was dry and uninhabited by the Lord, and you just couldn't play church anymore. The work I steward, called "The Wine Cellar," is plum full of people that were unwelcome or unhappy *elsewhere*, and they landed here. Don't feel disjointed. The Lord is causing these unsettled waters. He is doing a regional work in every area. The nomads will soon be brought together, and even now they are coming together in a wave of house churches that are springing up all over the place. Eventually there will be regional worship outlets where they will be able to gather corporately for large worship events. I believe that the Gate Beautiful bridal shower revivals will follow shortly thereafter.

Chapter 4 Questions

1. The Gideon Army is not limited to worship leaders, musicians, and intercessors. Although intercessors can be an exclusive breed in certain circles of intensity and focus, you too can be an effective intercessor at any level. Furthermore, let's put an end to the false idea that in order to have a ministry of worship, you must be a musician. As I just explained earlier in this study guide, it is when the crowd gathered for worship takes over, and the band becomes a mere ignition spark, that true unified corporate power is released. With this in mind, do you believe you are called to participate in the battles ahead with the Gideon Army?

   If yes, explain your heart.

   If no, explain your heart.

2. What is the first great responsibility of the Gideon Army?

   Why?

3. What is the next and *equally* great responsibility of the Gideon Army?

   Why?

4. Do you come from a church that is sleeping and your heart cries out for them?
   What can you do to help awaken the sleeping beauty?

5. What has been prophesied over you that you bear witness with in the Spirit?

   How can you participate with this word in faith to quicken its manifestation?

Chapter 4 Answers

1. Many are called, but few are chosen. Again, this is a personal decision. To choose or not to choose, that is the question. The great thing about the qualifications for service in this army is this: all you need to be is a lover of Jesus and a lover of truth! Jesus is truth personified, and He shall be seen over us in these radical times of the Gate Beautiful revivals. Even with these basic qualifications, this army will still be a remnant. As massive as the Church is, only a remnant will choose this life. However, when all is said and done, we will *all* be changed into perfected vessels of glory!

2. Our job is to tear down altars of religion, to *"cut asunder and to hew down"* the religious spirit and to build an altar of human hearts that will worship the Lord in spirit and in truth. Why? As we discovered just a short while ago, we don't want to fry our launching pad with religion and fall to the ground useless. How will we ever realize a harvest that way?

3. Our job is to worship in spirit and in truth, to reap a harvest in the *wine press* of the Holy Spirit so that the new wine of Heaven will be the first and lasting impression of Heaven for every new believer. Why? The harvest will be protected under the umbrella of the anointing of the Holy Spirit. So many in the past have been saved by hearing doctrine. Their hearts were pricked and they received the truth and were saved; but afterward they were integrated by a spirit of works and religion, and they were robbed of the true joy of the Lord's salvation. These Gate Beautiful revivals leave no room for any of the Uzzah's of our day to stand in the way of God being God. He fully intends to rock the boat and tip it over! Gather yourself together, and get ready for a ride that will shake the nations!

4. Many people attend a church that is asleep, and they don't even know it. Those that *do* know what is going on grieve. Their hearts cry out to Abba for the revelation of the living Jesus to capture their hearts. If this is you, you just became qualified as an intercessor with an anointing like Anna of the temple. It is profound what an intercessor can accomplish behind the scenes. Anna saw the redemption of the Lord manifest before her very eyes, just like Simeon. Unlike Anna, you won't have to wait 84 years to see the result of your intercession. Persevere with faith that is not of your own, but is the gift of God. Tarry till the Lord has you move on or till the Lord brings the victory. Either way, God will not forget your prayers because his word says that His watchmen bring Him remembrance (see Is. 62:6). His word will not return to Him void (see Is. 55:11), and you *are* the manifestation of His word (see 2 Cor. 3:3). Your intercession was born from *His* heart in the first place. It's a win-win situation, all the way around! Chew on that for a little while before you move on to the next answer. In other words, *selah*.

5. There are three ways to help your prophecy to come to pass. First, obey His word in the Bible. This is an implied condition. Second, believe that God spoke the prophecy through the prophet. Third, act with faith according to the word which was spoken. For instance, if you are supposed to heal the sick, then get your hands on some sick people and start doing it. The prophecy will come to pass with these things in place. All this will take place in steps over a period of time. Your faith muscles *will* be tested.

Study Guide

Chapter 5 Questions

1. What is your revelation of the Lord Jesus? Start writing:

Below.

Study Guide

Chapter 5 Questions

1. What is your revelation of the Lord Jesus? Start writing:

131

Chapter 5 Answers

1. The revelation that we have of the Lord in our spirits is the Lord we know. We can only worship who we know. Head knowledge of what Scripture says gives us *as believers* the ability to pine after true experiential knowledge. But we cannot worship someone we have never met or had experience with, no more than we can consummate with a spouse we have never met. We can only dream of it. Therefore, the most important thing in life is to *know Christ* so that He may be worshiped. However, one is not reconciled as a believer according to experiential knowledge, because *growing* in the knowledge of our Lord comes *after* salvation. We are saved by grace, not experience. Many *believers* have never been baptized in the Holy Spirit at all. Having been baptized in the Holy Spirit is *not* a pre-requisite to being saved. Speaking in tongues is *not* a pre-requisite to being saved either. Speaking in tongues is an *evidence* of salvation and also an evidence of being baptized in the Holy Spirit. I say all this to destroy the doctrine of demons that would have true believers petrified that they are not saved for lack of experience.

Every believer has varying degrees of spiritual experience with the Lord. There is no single person that has *one up* on another because their experience is more expansive. The Lord is no respecter of persons, and He loves each one of us equally. If you believe in the Lord Jesus, pray for the Holy Spirit to reveal Him in your spirit man. Your blessed assurance is already revealed to you in His word. Now, diligently seek the experiential knowledge of Jesus, so that the Scriptures will come alive in your spirit man. If you are a believer, then you *have heard* His voice. You may need to be *trained* (by the Holy Spirit) *in knowing* this voice and *recognizing it*, but you have *indeed heard it*. Seek Him, and you will find Him. He will *see to it* that you learn to discern His voice. If you have had any visions that sparked revelation inside of you, then chronicle those in your spirit. Meditate on the Scriptures, and ponder your experiences alongside of them. The Lord will always give you Scriptures to validate a vision or a prophetic experience of any kind. As you seek the Lord diligently in this way, you will begin to have greater and greater experiences. The Bible says that He rewards those that diligently seek Him (see Prov. 8:17). Therefore, seek the Lord!

Chapter 6 Questions

Here's a no-brainer. Chronicle all the violation that you have suffered from the enemy here, then use the worship tools described in this chapter to take back with violence that which the enemy has stolen from you.

1. Have you ever experienced, in any way, any of the manifestations mentioned in this chapter?

   If yes, explain:

2. Have you ever been frustrated by the manifestations demonstrated by others? (I will answer any questions you may have concerning these things; use my Website).

   If yes, explain what the root of this frustration was.

Chapter 6 Answers

Do not manifest in your flesh to conjure up some carnal resemblance of these worship manifestations. Let the Holy Spirit lead you in your quest to worship Jesus in spirit and in truth. The devil won't be fooled by carnal imitations. Carnality is the devil's play ground. I say this because I want to protect my readers that may not have *experienced* the kind of power in worship that is described in this chapter. This goes right along with what we just discussed concerning the revelation of the Lord and having experiential knowledge. Begin by worshiping the Lord according to the present revelation you have, and then beseech Him with *great* desire for more. He longs to pour out more and more of His Spirit for you. Be increasingly hungry, for those who hunger shall be filled. Be increasingly thirsty, for those who thirst shall be satisfied. You *will* be satisfied, but the Lord has more. Long for more! Never stop being hungry or thirsty for more of Jesus. You will never exhaust His capacity to fill you again as if you've never been filled before.

We are on an eternal journey of discovering the lover who will never be fully realized. He will always leave us longing for more. That is the most wonderful thing. In the natural, many people seem to grow well-acquainted with their spouses, leaving them with a vacuum for unfulfilled romance. This will never be the case with Jesus! Longing for Him is the reason that receiving Him is so satisfying! Your desire must be for *Him* specifically, and not for the payback the devil owes you. Payback is already guaranteed in Scripture. Worship is to be given to the Lord unhindered by any other desire. Eventually, as you begin to grow in worship, you will soon discover the Lord's habitation with you. This is true for every believer. If you already have power encounters with Jesus, this does not exempt you from going deeper, wider, and higher. The worshiper who is satisfied with the same level of communion with Jesus as they had yesterday, will soon extinguish that flame.

Chapter 7 Questions

1. Did you attend any gatherings when the Toronto Blessing or Brownsville revivals were aflame? (I will answer any questions you may have concerning these things; use my Website).

If yes, what were your observations?

Chapter 9 Questions

(Note: There are no questions for Chapter 8.)

*For this we declare to you by the Lord's [own] word, that we who are alive and remain until the coming of the Lord **shall in no way precede [into His presence]** or have any advantage at all over those who have previously fallen asleep [in Him in death]. For the Lord Himself will descend from heaven with a loud cry of summons, with the shout of an archangel, and with the blast of the trumpet of God. And those who have departed this life in Christ **will rise first. Then we, the living ones who remain [on the earth], shall simultaneously be caught up** along with [the resurrected dead] in the clouds to meet the Lord in the air; and so always (through the eternity of the eternities) we shall be with the Lord* (1 Thessalonians 4:15-17).

1. What does this Scripture mean to you? This question does not deal with the definition of the words "to meet with the Lord in the air," because we already covered what Scripture has to say about all that in the chapter. Dig deeper. Look at the bold phrases especially. I pray that it won't create discord among you. Be open to hear what the Scriptures really say about this subject, and refuse to get into debates that are unhealthy and unspiritual. As a group, work together, and look up all the scriptures that pertain to the thoughts contained in this one Scripture. Do a word study, do a very thorough study together. Dig deep until you have exhausted it. (I will answer any questions you may have concerning these things; use my Website).

Use the next page to write your interpretations of this Scripture.

2.   What does this chapter declare that is a contrary theme to movies like the *Left Behind* series, or other apocalyptic movies like it? What does our study of the Bible reveal that is in direct conflict with the doctrine these movies teach?

Once again, be tender with one another. There are a lot of ill-informed teachings out there that the Body of Christ at large has adopted as being biblical, simply because they never studied the subject for themselves. Please be kind with one another as you go through all of this. This chapter has merely skimmed the surface of what the Bible has to say about the end-times and the Day of the Lord, which are really two different events. It is my style to use literal definitions of the original language and not raw and pale interpretations of words used in the English translation. Often times, English words do not mean what they seem to imply and do not have the depth or color of the Greek and Hebrew. There are some instances where interpretation can come into play concerning the theme of what the literal definition of the language in Scripture is saying; but if the understanding of original language is not defined, you won't have a platform to create an interpretation of the intent of the words in the first place. I don't want to be guilty of giving an uninformed opinion. God's opinion works for me! *Please*, let it work for you as well. Make sure that you understand what you have studied before you make a stand on any issue, and then make all of your declarations with great love and tenderness!

Write your answers on the next page. (I will answer any questions you may have concerning these things; use my Website.)

Chapter 10 Questions

1. Have you had any visitations from the Lord?

    If yes, how can you use the message within the visitation to bless the Body of Christ?

2. If you have not had any specific visitations of the Lord, what kind of experience can you share that can be used to glorify Him and prepare the Bride for the future?

    Be sure to ask the Lord for Scriptures that validate your interpretation of your experience, and look up the definitions of key words in the original language. God will *always* validate a prophetic experience that you have with His word. If your interpretation of the experience cannot be found in Scripture *after* seeking out the original language, then keep seeking the Lord for the true interpretation. He *will* answer. God richly bless you in the wonderful name of Jesus Christ!

Chronological Chart

On the next two pages is a chronological calendar of events that is based upon Scripture. The verse references are included. The chart sets biblical events in their chronological order. The events included are those which are best suited to give proper understanding to the landmarks of redemptive history that we discussed in chapter eight.

EVENT	YEARS FROM CREATION	YEAR OF EVENT	YEARS UNTIL NEXT EVENT	SCRIPTURE OF NEXT EVENT
CREATION FIRST ADAM	0	3950 B.C.	1056	GENESIS 5:28-29
NOAH'S BIRTH	1056	2894 B.C.	600	GENESIS 7:11
BEGINNING OF FLOOD	1656	2294 B.C.	293	GENESIS 11:26
BIRTH OF ABRAHAM	1949	2001 B.C.	941	2 SAMUEL 5:3
DAVID BEGINS REIGN	2890	1060 B.C.	44	1 KINGS 6:1
SOLOMON BUILDS TEMPLE	2934	1016 B.C.	428	2 KINGS 25:8-9
FIRST TEMPLE DESTROYED	3362	588 B.C.	582	MATTHEW 2:1

Chronological Chart

EVENT	YEARS FROM CREATION	YEAR OF EVENT	YEARS UNTIL NEXT EVENT	SCRIPTURE OF NEXT EVENT
BIRTH OF JESUS	3944	6 B.C.	35	LUKE 3:23
CHRIST'S MINISTRY BEGINS	3979	A.D. 29	3	LUKE 23:33
CHRIST'S CRUCIFIXION	3982	A.D. 32	5	ACTS 9:1-16
CALL OF THE APOSTLE PAUL	3987	A.D. 37	33	LUKE 21:5-6; MATTHEW 24:15-16
SECOND TEMPLE DESTROYED	4020	A.D. 70	1924	ACTS 3:19–21
TORONTO BLESSING AND OTHER REVIVALS	5944	A.D. 1994...	?	GATE BEAUTIFUL REVIVALS PENDING

Endnotes

Preface

1. *Webster's New Collegiate Dictionary*, 7th edition, s.v. "religious."

2. Danny Steyne, November 1982.

Chapter 1

1. "The Call" is a powerful annual event hosted by Prophet Lou Engle that focuses on prayer and fasting and gathers worshipers together in a public area to worship and seek the Lord for revival.

2. *Strong's Exhaustive Concordance of the Bible*, Greek #5611 from #5610, s.v. "horaios" (beautiful).

3. Lynn Swann is a NFL Hall of Fame football player (wide receiver) whose extraordinary talent for making receptions rivaled all other receivers of his day, and for that matter, of this day as well. For more information see http://en.wikipedia.org/wiki/Lynn_Swann.

Chapter 2

1. *Strong's Exhaustive Concordance of the Bible*, Hebrew #41, s.v. "Abinadab."

2. *Ibid.*, Hebrew #1184, s.v. "Baale."

3. *Ibid.*, Hebrew #2982, s.v. "Jebus."

4. *Ibid.*, Hebrew #319, s.v. "posterity."

5. *Ibid.*, Hebrew #1755, s.v. "posterity."

6. *Webster's New Collegiate Dictionary*, 7th edition, s.v. "posterity."

Chapter 3

1. *Strong's Exhaustive Concordance of the Bible*, Hebrew #1984, s.v. "halal."

2. The Toronto Blessing began in 1994 while Randy Clark was ministering at the Toronto Airport Christian Fellowship, pastured by John and Carol Arnott. Many in the broader Church were offended by the Toronto revival because of the strange Holy Spirit physical manifestations that people experience there. The outpouring of the Holy Spirit continues there and has brought much of the Church into radical reformation. To this day, the Church is being affected by the power that was released. For more information, visit the church Website at http://www.tacf.org/.

Chapter 4

1. *Strong's Exhaustive Concordance of the Bible*, Hebrew #4066, s.v. "Midian."

2. *Ibid.*, Greek #2215, s.v. "tares."

3. *Ibid.*, Hebrew #1438, s.v. "Gideon."

4. *Ibid.*, Greek #32 and 34, s.v. "angels."

5. *Ibid.*, Hebrew #8138, s.v. "second."

6. *Ibid.*, Hebrew #7886, s.v. "Shiloh."

7. *Ibid.*, Hebrew #3034, s.v. "Judah."

Chapter 5

1. *Strong's Exhaustive Concordance of the Bible*, Greek #3516, s.v. "babes and sucklings."

2. *Ibid.*, Greek #136, s.v. "praise."

Chapter 6

1. *Strong's Exhaustive Concordance of the Bible*, Hebrew #1523 s.v. "guwl" (rejoice).

2. *Webster's New Collegiate Dictionary*, 7th edition, s.v. "violent."

3. *Ibid.*, s.v. "rejoice."

4. *Strong's Exhaustive Concordance of the Bible*, Greek #973 from #971.

5. *Ibid.*, Hebrew #1984, s.v. "halal" (praise).

6. *Ibid.*, Hebrew #7442, s.v. "ranan" (sing).

7. *Webster's New Collegiate Dictionary*, 7th edition, s.v. "rage."

8. *Strong's Exhaustive Concordance of the Bible*, Hebrew #4294.

9. *Ibid.*, Hebrew #5608, s.v. "sapphires."

10. *Webster's New Collegiate Dictionary*, 7th edition, s.v. "commune."

11. *Strong's Exhaustive Concordance of the Bible*, Hebrew #4578, s.v. "belly."

12. Rick Joyner, *The Final Quest* (Fort Mill, SC: Morningstar Publishers, 2006) 61-62. Used by permission.

Chapter 7

1. *Strong's Exhaustive Concordance of the Bible,* Greek #5614, s.v. "hosanna."

2. *Ibid.*, Hebrew #3467, s.v. "hosanna."

3. *Webster's New Collegiate Dictionary*, 7th edition, s.v. "perfection."

Chapter 9

1. *Strong's Exhaustive Concordance of the Bible*, Greek #109, "aer" (air).

2. *Webster's New Collegiate Dictionary*, 7th edition, s.v. "circumambient."

3. *Webster's New Collegiate Dictionary*, 7th edition, s.v. "consume."

4. *Ibid.*, s.v. "induction."

5. *Strong's Exhaustive Concordance of the Bible*, Hebrew #5645, s.v. "awb" (cloud).

6. *Webster's New Collegiate Dictionary*, 7th edition, s.v. (see full) "fullness."

7. *Strong's Exhaustive Concordance of the Bible*, Greek #5048, s.v. "teleloo" (perfected).

8. Our beloved five-fold evangelists are sending reports regularly of the miracles of God occurring, especially in third world countries. Two men that endorsed this book, Wayne C. Anderson and Brian Simmons, are blessed with the testimony of having seen Christ raise the dead through their ministries.

Chapter 10

1. That the Lord will visit people in bodily form has been prophesied by Danny Steyne and many others.

2. Danny Steyne, Irving King, and many others have experienced physical encounters with Jesus.

3. *Strong's Exhaustive Concordance of the Bible*, Hebrew #1697 & #2896 s.v. "dabar" (good matter) (word).

Glossary of Definitions
(in order of appearance)

Beautiful (Acts 3:2)

Greek Strong's #5611 from #5610

Horaios #5611

Belonging to the right hour or season (timely), i.e. (by implication) flourishing (beauteous [figuratively]):

KJV—beautiful

Hora #5610

Apparently a primary word; an "hour" (literally or figuratively):

KJV—day, hour, instant, season, short, [even-] tide, (high) time.

Abinadab (2 Samuel 6:1-3)

Heb. Strong's #41 from #5068 the prime root

Abiynadab/nadab #5068

KJV—offer freely, be (give, make, offer self) willing (-ly).

To volunteer (as a soldier), to present spontaneously

Baale (2 Samuel 6:2)

    From Heb. Strong's #1184

A` aley Yehuwdah

    Masters of Judah; Baale-Jehudah, also, a place in Palestine

Jebusite (2 Chronicles 3:1)

    From the Heb. Strong's #2983 from 2982

Yebuwc #2982

    Trodden, i.e. threshing-place; Jebus, the aboriginal name of Jerusalem:

    KJV—Jebu

Posterity (1 Chronicles 17:10b–12)

    Heb. Strong's # 319

Achariyth

    The last or end, hence, the future; also posterity:

    KJV—(last, latter) end (time), hinder (utter) -most, length, posterity, remnant,

    residue, reward

    Also, Heb. Strong's #1755

dowr

    Properly, a revolution of time, i.e. an age or generation; also a dwelling:

    KJV—age, evermore, generation,

    [n-] ever, posterity

Posterity

    Websters:

        The offspring of one progenitor to the furthest generation and all future generations

Glossary of Definitions

Midianite (Judges 6:3-4)

> From the Heb. Strong's 4066

Madown

> KJV—brawling, contention (-ous), discord, strife. Compare.
> There are many variations of this word, each of which gives
> a similar definition.

Tares (Matthew 13:30 KJV)

> From the Greek. Strong's 2215

Zizanion

> Of uncertain origin; darnel or false grain:
> KJV—tares

Gideon

> From the Heb. Strong's 1439 from 1438

Gada 1438

> A primitive root; to fell a tree; generally, to destroy
> anything:
> KJV—cut (asunder, in sunder, down, off),
> hew down

Angels (Matthew 13:39)

> From the Greek Strong's 32 from 34

Aggelos

> (To bring tidings); a messenger; especially an "angel"; by
> implication, a pastor:
> Compare # 34 a drove: KJV—herd

Shiloh (Genesis 49:10)

> From the Heb. Strong's #7886

Shiyloh

Tranquil; Shiloh, an epithet of the Messiah:

KJV—Shiloh

Judah (Psalms 114:2)

From Heb. Strong's #3063 from 3034

Yadah #3034

A primitive root: Literally, to use (i.e. hold out) the hand; physically, to throw (a stone, an arrow) at or away; especially to revere or worship (with extended hands); intensively, to bemoan (by wringing the hands):

KJV—cast (out), (make) confess (-ion), praise, shoot, (give) thanks-giving)

Babes (Matthew 21:16)

From Greek Strong's #3516

Nepios

Figuratively, a simple-minded person, an immature Christian

Praise (Matthew 21:16)

From Greek Strong's #136

Ainos

Apparently a prime word; properly, *a story*, but used in the sense of Greek #1868; praise (of God):

KJV—praise

Rejoice (Psalms 9:14)

From Heb. Strong's #1523

Guwl

A primitive root; properly, to spin round (under the influence of any violent emotion), i.e. usually rejoice:

KJV—be glad, joy, be joyful, rejoice

Glossary of Definitions

Violent and violence
>   (Mathew 11:12b)
>   From Greek Strong's #973 from #971

Biastes #973
>   A forcer, i.e. (figuratively) energetic:
>   KJV—violent

Biazo #971
>   To force, i.e. (reflexively) to crowd oneself (into), or (passively) to be seized:
>   KJV—press, suffer violence

Praise (Psalms 149:1 KJV)
>   From Heb. Strong's #1984

Halal
>   A primitive root; to be clear (orig. of sound, but usually of color); to shine; hence, to make a show, to boast; and thus to be (clamorously) foolish; to rave; causatively, to celebrate;
>   also to stultify:
>   KJV—(make) boast (self), celebrate, commend, (deal, make), fool (-ish, -ly), glory, give [light], be (make, feign mad) (against), give in marriage, [sing, be worthy of] praise, rage, renowned, shine

Sing (Psalms 149:5)
>   From Heb. Strong's #7442.

Ranan
>   A primitive root; properly, to creak
>   (or emit a stridulous sound),
>   i.e. to shout (usually for joy):
>   KJV—aloud for joy, cry out, be joyful (greatly, make to) rejoice, (cause to) shout (for joy), (cause to) sing (aloud, for joy, out), triumph

Rod (Psalms 110:2)

From Heb. Strong's #4294

Matteh

A *branch* (as extending); figuratively, a tribe; also a rod, whether for chastising (figuratively, correction), ruling (a sceptre), throwing (a lance), or walking (a staff; figuratively, a support of life, e. g. carrier of bread):

KJV—rod, staff, tribe

Sapphire (Ezekiel 1:26)

From Heb. Strong's #5601 from #5608

Cappiyr # 5601

A gem (perhaps used for scratching other substances), probably the sapphire:

KJV—sapphire

Caphar #5608

A primitive root; properly, to score with a mark as a tally or record, i.e. (by implication) to inscribe, and also to enumerate; intensively, to recount, i.e. celebrate:

KJV—*commune*, (ac-) count; *declare*, number, penknife, reckon, scribe, *shew forth*, speak, talk, *tell* (*out*), writer

Body/Belly (Song of Songs 5:14b)

Heb. Strong's #4578

Me` ah

From an unused root probably meaning to be soft; used only in plural the intestines, or (collectively) the abdomen, figuratively, sympathy; by implication, a vest; by extents the stomach, the uterus (or of men, the seat of generation), the heart (figuratively):

KJV—belly, bowels, heart, womb

Glossary of Definitions

Hosanna

>Greek Strong's #5614

Hosanna

>Oh save! Hosanna (i.e. hoshia-na), an exclamation of adoration:
>
>KJV—hosanna

Perfection

>*Websters 7th New Collegiate Dictionary:*
>Flawlessness, saintliness, and an exemplification of supreme excellence

Air (1 Thessalonians 4:17)

>From Greek Strong's #109

Aer #109

>To breathe unconsciously, i.e. respire; by analogy, to blow; "air"
>
>(as naturally circumambient):
>
>KJV—air

Circumambient

>*Websters 7th New Collegiate Dictionary:*
>Surround in a circle, surrounding or encompassing

Induction

>*Websters 7th New Collegiate Dictionary:*
>The act or process of reasoning from a part to a whole, from the individual to the universal. Also the process by which an electrical conductor becomes electrified when near a charged body, by which a magnetizable body, becomes magnetized when in a magnetic field, or in the magnetic flux, set up by a magneto-motive force

Cloud (1 Kings 18:44)

    From Heb. Strong's #5645

Ab

    Properly, an envelope, i.e. darkness (or density, 2 Chronicles 4:17); specifically, a (scud) cloud;

    KJV—clay, (thick) cloud, thick, thicket like clay

Perfected

    From Greek Strong's #5048

Teleioo

    To complete, i.e. (literally) accomplish, or (figuratively) consummate (in character):

    KJV—consecrate, finish, fulfill, make) perfect.

Touching (Psalms 45:1)

    From Heb. Strongs #4639

Ma` aseh

    An action (good or bad); generally, a transaction; abstractly, activity; by implication, a product (specifically, a *poem*) or (generally) property:

    KJV—act, art, bakemeat, business, deed, do (-ing), *labor*, *thing made*, ware of making, occupation, thing offered, operation, possession, well, ([handy-, needle-, net-]) *work* (ing, *-manship*), wrought.

Good Matter (Psalms 45:1)

    From Heb. Strongs #1697 & #2896

#1697 *Dabar*

    A word; by implication, a matter (as spoken of) or thing; adverbially, a cause:

Glossary of Definitions

#2896 *Towb*

> Good (as an adjective) in the widest sense; used likewise as
> a noun, both in the masculine and the feminine, the
> singular and the plural (good, a good or good thing, *a*
> *good man* or woman; the good, goods or good things,
> good men or women), also as an adverb (well):

> KJV—beautiful, best, better, bountiful, cheerful, at ease, fair
> (word), (be in) favour, fine, glad, good, graciously, joy-
> ful, kindly, kindness, liketh (best), loving, merry, most,
> pleasant, pleaseth, pleasure, precious, prosperity, ready,
> sweet, wealth, welfare, (be) well ([-favoured]).

Index

Ephraim: a multitude of nations
    Genesis 48:19

David retrieves the Ark from Abinadab's house
    2 Samuel 6:1

Today's Abinadab's releasing the sons of David
    Malachi 4:6 NKJV

Don't try to make the anointing of God palatable to the flesh
    2 Samuel 6:6-7

Release the Levites
    Psalms 110:3

David sacrifices on Mount Moriah
    1 Chronicles 21,18-19

Solomon builds the Temple
    2 Chronicles 3:1

24/7 Worship and Prayer
    Isaiah 62:6-7
    Luke 18:7 KJV

The rule and reign of Jesus prophesied
    1 Chronicles 17:10b-12

Perpetrators of religion and the jezebel spirit
    Jude 4,12

Radical, public and corporate worship
    Zechariah 9:13-15

The song of the terminally unsatisfied who always seeks more
    Luke 6:21

Israel punished for fearing false God's
    Judges 6:3-4

Gideon's army set apart
    Judges 7:5-7

Index

The Lord thunders through His worshipers
Joel 3:16

The Lord is enthroned upon the worship of His people
Ezekiel 1:26

His blood flows through spiritual worship
Song of Songs 5:14b

Restoration of the nations
Jeremiah 12:15

Times of refreshing
Acts 3:19-20 KJV

Lucifer fell without temptation
Ezekiel 28:15

Stumbling into forbidden knowledge (the Masters' plan unfolds)
Genesis 3:22

Going from glory to glory
2 Corinthians 3:18

A millennial day
2 Peter 3:8b

Noah: a shadow of the end times
Luke 17:26

The very first act of worship was performed by Abraham and
Isaac and foreshadowed the cross of Christ on the same
Mountain top where the temple was built by Solomon
Genesis 22:2-4

Jesus said, "Your father Abraham rejoiced to see my day: and he
saw it, and was glad". This is the third day; the day of which
the Lord was speaking
Luke 13:32; John 8:56 KJV

Index

Since we are in Him and He is in us, we have supreme authority as bond servants to declare the decree's of the King in the land and literally come bearing His name.

John 17:20-23

God's wisdom and power shall be made known to all through the Church

Ephesians 3:9-11

All things come from God and shall be reconciled back to God

Colossians 1:16-17,20

At the last trump the secrets of the Lord will be revealed before His glorious return

Revelation 10:5-7

Jesus *is* really the worship leader

Hebrews 2:12

The Father speaks concerning the King (Jesus) through whom all things came (see Glossary of this Scripture)

Psalm 45:1

Jesus rejoices in His inhabited world before the Father, and before creation was complete.

Proverbs 8:30-31

The very joy of Jesus is our strength to stand in righteousness

Psalms 45 6-7 NKJV

A picture of the latter rain harvest

Psalms 45:10-17 NKJV

The Bride offers her love to the King in His harvest fields, and beckons Him to hasten the day. Let us go out *early* she says

Song of Songs 7:11-12

Ministry Contact Information

To invite David and Judith Harris to minister at your church or event please e-mail them at shekinahministries@cox.net.

Wayne C. & Irene Joy Anderson
Standsure Ministries

Wayne C. Anderson is an anointed voice of divine healing and a prophetic/revelatory voice to this generation. He and his wife, Irene, are founders of Standsure Ministries. Together they passionately seek the tangible manifestation of the ministry of Jesus on this earth today!

With the heart of a father, Wayne gives apostolic oversight to hundreds of pastors, ministers, and churches in the United States and on five continents. He is the Apostolic Director and co-founder of the International Apostolic Ministries (I.A.M.) and has established a rapidly growing movement toward reformation and church planting.

Wayne is a Revivalist who has been intimately involved with numerous local and international revivals. He is a founding minister of the Seattle Revival Center and was President of the John G. Lake organization of ministries for five years.

For information about the ministry of
Wayne C. & Irene Joy Anderson
visit www.Standsure.net.

Multiple Resources available by Wayne Anderson on:
Healing! The Table of the Lord, Heaven,
Living a Miraculous Life, The Anointing,
Financial Reformation, Baptism,
Leadership Training & Team Building,
Faith, The Power of Prayer,
and more!

Order online at www.Standsure.net

For catalog requests contact:
Standsure Ministries
P.O. Box 174, Meridian, ID 83680
StandsureMinistries@Standsure.net

Chad Taylor
Consuming Fire Revival Network

What makes Chad's appeal for revival unique is that he has *seen* and *experienced* revival which has resulted in entire regions and cities coming under the presence of God for months and even years at a time, seeing thousands of salvations. If your church is ready to embrace the revival that these times demand, Chad Taylor brings a clarion call, or namely this; REVIVAL!

Chad is also the author of the book *Why Revival Still Tarries* which is already in its second printing and is being read worldwide.

For more information visit:

www.consumingfire.com.

the time has come

Mountain Of Worship

Danny Steyne

In 1987 I had a vision. I saw a flat plain that grew into a volcano and became a "Mountain of Worship" that exploded worship all over the region, the nation, and around the world. It was an event of passionate worship that resulted in exaltation, magnification, and praise of God in spirit and truth! It was full of God's power, and the miraculous power of God was released to all those in the shadow of the Mountain.

This "Mountain of Worship" is not simply another organization, it is not simply another noun on the "marketplace" of Christianity...it is an organism and a verb... passionate about bringing Glory to the Father through "much fruit...it is a "perpetual event of spirit and truth worship." It is a lifestyle of worship. It is a region...a nation...the world...abandoned to passionate holy worship...until every knee bows, every tongue tells, both the lost and the found, in Heaven and in hell...that Jesus is Lord!

Danny Steyne

If you would like Danny Steyne or a Mountain Of Worship Team to speak at your church, ministry, or conference, or if you have interest in Mountain Of Worship, MOWBooks, MOWMusic, MOWTeaching, MOWConferences, MOWSummits, MOWIntenships, or Mountain Of Worship Schools of Worship, Creativity, & Ministry, please contact us at the address below:

Mountain Of Worship
P.O. Box 212204
Columbia, SC 29221-2204
Telephone: 803-665-8990
www.MountainOfWorship.com
worship@mountainofworship.com